The 9 Great Lies Of Digital Marketing

I0464697

JIMMY CRANGLE

Jimmy Crangle

Copyright © 2016 Jimmy Crangle

All rights reserved.

ISBN:1523405031
ISBN-13:97815232405039

DEDICATION

To my lovely wife Da and our beautiful daughters Liz & Skye

Jimmy Crangle

CONTENTS

About Jimmy Crangle

ACKNOWLEDGMENTS

Special thanks to Perry Marshall for his excellent advice & support over the past 8 years, the Evil Bald Genius Jon McCulloch for his arse kicking, Chris Cardell for his excellent marketing seminars, Dan Kennedy for his profound marketing advice at the Sovereignty summit and of course to all my family & friends around the world.

Introduction

"A successful man is one who can lay a firm foundation with the bricks others have thrown at him" - David Brinkley

Back in the 1960s, there was a marketing expert in New York (I can't remember his name) who specialised in setting up lead-generation systems for doctors and chiropractors. He would set up a complete marketing system for each practice and aim to bring in 72 patients before moving on to a new project; his approach was based on a conclusion that any new practice needed 72 patients to be viable.

The question people always asked him was, "What is the single best thing you do to generate these 72 patients?"

"I don't know of any one thing I can do to bring in 72 patients," he would reply. "I do, however, know of 72 things I can do to bring in one patient… and I do all 72 of them."

This is profoundly brilliant advice.

Nowadays, everyone chases the FREE traffic, the MAGIC bullet, or the social media illusion. The truth is that you simply cannot build a legitimate business on free traffic or the latest fad. Business owners and entrepreneurs who do quickly find themselves at the mercy of search engine optimisation companies, social media reps, and finicky Google.

In fact, thousands of companies over the years have awoken to devastating profit losses overnight simply because their websites no longer ranked on the first page of Google – often with no logical reason for the drop in rankings. When a company relies too much on this one marketing channel, a drop from the top three listings can even mean going bust.

Your Biggest Marketing Obstacle…

Do you want to know the single biggest obstacle holding you back in business and in life?

YOU !

Much of what you have learnt about money, success, and marketing over the years is either false or misguided. In order to get where you want to be, you need to first unlearn the myths and conventional "wisdom" before you do anything else. You need to change your core beliefs before anything about your business reality will change.

And then you need the flexibility to keep changing those beliefs with evolving technologies and social norms. The marketing world is moving fast. Things have changed rapidly over the past five years or so, and the pace seems to pick up speed with every passing month. What worked online just a couple years ago may no longer work today, or it may have become so expensive that it's not worth the cost per new customer.

Everything I share with you in this book is based on my experiences and the experiences of other successful people. I don't just make this shit up.

But first, I want to expose some of the advertising and marketing lies being punted around to break some of your assumptions, many of which you may not even realise you're clinging to. I want to put an end to your frustration, anger, and fear – and that begins by recognising some of the big lies, myths, and misconceptions advocated by advertising reps, marketing agencies, SEO companies, other business owners, and even the well-meaning, but clueless, guys down at the pub.

So, Let's get started shall we?

Lie #1 - We Can Get Your Website to the #1 Spot On Google - *(The Big SEO Lie)*

SEO used to be a very important part of any online marketing strategy. But if you base your entire marketing strategy around SEO and hope that Google will send you free traffic forever, you're doomed to failure before you even start.

Not only is free search traffic not free but it's totally unreliable because it's completely outside of your control. No matter how good you are at SEO, or how much money you spend on your website, Google can slap you down a few pages on a whim, or remove you from its index altogether.

That means Google can put you out of business in a second, without any notice, and there's bugger all you can do about it! Remember this above all else – YOU CAN'T BUILD A BUSINESS ON FREE ADVERTISING!

And that is not to mention that most websites aren't even set up to deal with the avalanche of traffic promised by SEO companies. So, even if these smooth talkers delivered the holy grail of traffic, most business owners would fail to optimise because they don't have an opt-in and follow-up system in place to convert these visitors into customers.

The problem here is ego. Website owners want to be #1 to one-over their competitors. For a lot of these folks, being seen as #1 appears more important than actually converting visitors to customers!

Not to mention: just being #1 on Google and getting slammed with traffic does not necessarily mean an increase in more customers or more sales. In fact, it rarely happens in most industries, primarily because the free traffic on Google and other search engines is of such a poor quality.

And even if those top ranking spots were secure and dependable high-traffic positions, SEO companies couldn't be relied on to get your website there even for sexual favours … Because the top 4 spots are now always taken up by PPC (Pay per Click) ads – this has been the case for a while, so I'm not sure how these guys still get away with their claims.

This means that #1 on the organic listings is actually #5 on the search page. A convenient lie you'll hear from SEO companies to ease your mind on this is that "no-one clicks on those PPC ads." Oh, really? Is that why Google makes billions of dollars every month from people clicking on those ads?

In fact, I recently tried an experiment with a small group of clients at one of our meetings. I watched them run a search on Google, click on PPC ads, and then later deny point-blank that they clicked on the ads at all! It's very subliminal. If the message is relevant to the search, most people will click on the PPC ad without even thinking about what they're doing.

If you want to cut through the bull, stop thinking about "more traffic" and instead start thinking about "higher conversions." It has become virtually impossible nowadays to get an immediate sale from a first-time website visit, so don't try to sell anything at first. Instead, focus on becoming a problem-solver for your visitors.

The secret of success is to use your online page as a tool to build a database of prospects. To do that, your website must be designed to convert visitors into prospects, and then you need qualified traffic. From there, you can build trust by providing quality information so that they will be more likely to buy from you when the time is right.

SEO Is Dead

I predicted back in 2014 that 'SEO' free traffic days were numbered. In the future, virtually all of Google's "free" listings will become pay-per-click. The shaded area behind the sponsored ads has disappeared, removing the main distinction between sponsored ads and organic listings.

The Google Adwords system has become very sophisticated, and Google now has much more control over the quality of the PPC listings than the organic search listings. PPC ads must meet strict criteria, and merchants are not allowed to advertise porn, gambling, or get-rich-quick programs.

Your website has already been given a quality score by Google. Your click-through-rate (CTR), quality score, ad relevance, and website landing page will determine not only how much you pay per click but whether your ads will be shown at all.

All of this is actually good news for Google's customers (users searching Google for information), as well as advertisers who know what they are doing. And Google stands to make billions of dollars in profit, so it's great for the company behind it all too.

The point is that no SEO company can guarantee you results, or even guarantee you financial results if they do get you ranking results, and yet you still have to pay the work they do if you buy their pitch. Save yourself valuable time, money, and frustration and forget about SEO. The "free traffic" days are coming to an end.

UK marketing guru Chris Cardell said this at a recent marketing seminar I attended:

"If you're into SEO (Search Engine Optimisation) and getting high up on the free listings on Google, try this...Get a mobile phone, go onto the internet, go to Google, and search for 'digital camera.' Look at the results.

"Depending on the size of the screen you're on, either all or most of your screen will be filled with paid results - ads. They don't look like it because the shading behind the Google ads is almost impossible to see on a mobile, but they're ads.

"You won't see the free listings unless you scroll down the page. And most people don't scroll down the page. So many mobile users are no longer seeing the free listings.

"Now, jump a few years into the future, when the majority of searches will be on mobile devices, and answer this question... What's the point of SEO?

"There won't be any point. And quite honestly, there's very little point now. One of the things I'm most proud of over the last ten years is that I never gave in to the temptation to do a course on Search Engine Optimisation. It would have been an instant source of additional profit for my business because everybody loves the next new thing. We showed business owners how to do it as part of other courses - and it was worth doing, within reason, but those days are coming to an end.

"This is controversial - and some of those who make money selling SEO will rant and rave about me - but I don't care. Of all the BS I've heard over the last ten years, I don't think anything comes close to the empty promises of the SEO world. It rarely worked very well. It's working particularly badly now. And soon it won't work at all.

"So that's the blunt truth: Your business is not going to get an endless stream of customers from the free listings on Google. It ain't happening. Which means we need to get very smart at getting your customers from other sources." Source - Chris Cardell, www.CardellMedia.co.uk

I still get spam emails from SEO companies desperately looking for new customers. If they're really so good at what they do, and if SEO is so important for MY business, then why must they resort to spamming in order to get business? Surely they must already be #1 on Google and bringing in the tonnes of traffic they're promising me.

If something smells like bullshit, it usually is.

Lie #2 - You Need a Professional-Looking Website

This lie costs business owners MILLIONS in unnecessary web design fees, lost opportunities, and wasted advertising spend. One of my clients spent GB£9,643 on a new state-of-the art website that took several months to complete. The website looked great, but it didn't convert any visitors into customers. She essentially paid almost 10 grand for an online brochure that didn't work!

Again, this is an EGO thing. It's human nature to want to impress your peers, to "be seen," to be doing better than your competitors, and to look the part. The bottom line is this, though – how much money is your website bringing in?

You can build a website for next to nothing nowadays. I personally use a free web design platform because it's fast, easy to use, and I have complete control. The last website I built brought in just under £400,000 in a couple of months. It cost me around £60 per year in hosting fees and bugger all to build it.

To be honest, I only did this after I had wasted nearly £6,000 in fees I paid to so-called web designers! There are plenty of free web design platforms you can take advantage of. Regardless of which platform you use, maintain control of your website design, functionality, operation, publishing, and most of all ... conversion strategy! Try www.eclickfunnels.com, Instapage or Unbounce which have excellent A/B split testers.

Here some of the secrets of my online success:

Every piece of advertising, webpage, sales letter, brochure, or banner ad that you send out MUST include ALL of these ingredients:

- A powerful headline that commands attention
- An emotionally provocative, benefit-driven message that states your USP (unique selling proposition).
- A compelling call to action. Offer something valuable in return for contact details.
- A series of automated, follow-up emails for building long-term trust with your prospects.

Look at it like this. A website is a powerful media tool that MUST be designed to solve problems quickly for people who are searching for solutions. It also must be designed to convert those searchers into leads. Your follow-up system – which may consist of emails, telemarketing, direct mail, or a combination of these – should then convert them into customers.

Lie #3 - The Internet Is Different From All Other Media

Many people believe the internet is so different from other media platforms that a completely different approach is required. Or, that their business/industry is somehow unique. Wrong! It really amazes me how those who have never even so much as read an eBook on marketing start a business with such deeply-rooted opinions of what does and doesn't work. Conventional wisdom is rife.

While we're on the subject of opinions, let me expose five BIG false opinions before we move on. These are the main objections I still get from my clients.

False Opinion #1 – "Businesses/Corporations Won't Respond to This Direct Response Marketing."

Businesses don't actually buy things, believe it or not; they never have, and they never will. PEOPLE buy things ... human beings. The same emotional creatures buy things on the internet for EXACTLY the same fundamental reasons they did at the local market 2,000 years ago. The only thing that has changed are the tools and media we use.

False Opinion #2 - "I Just want to Run an Internet Business."

Stop and think about this for a second ... There's really no such thing as an internet business. If you advertise in a newspaper, does that mean you have a newspaper business? Or a Yellow Pages business?

The internet is an advanced medium, a fantastic lead generation and delivery tool ... if used properly! Those who think they have an "internet business" have gone bust or they will go bust. Always remember that you're still dealing with real human beings, not computers.

False Opinion #3 - "I'm Entitled to My Own Opinion."

When it comes to building a successful business, your opinions and beliefs don't count. The opinions of your friends, family, spouse, other business owners, and the guy down at the pub … DON'T matter. What works, works. Why does it work? Doesn't matter.

Don't take advice from well-intentioned people who really don't know what they're talking about. It's one of the biggest mistakes people make in life. And most of the information out there about making money online is complete crap.

False Opinion #4 - "I Lost Money Before; I'm Not Cut Out For This."

Successful entrepreneurs learn from mistakes. They make mistakes, and they keep learning. In contrast, those who fail in business and life consider their errors bad luck or blame others.

Keep learning and never give up!

False Opinion #5 – "You Need to Be Lucky To Be Successful Online."

Your success depends on your attitude, a burning desire to succeed, and whether you're prepared to learn the skills necessary to succeed in your business. Get prepared by learning as much as you can about online marketing, as well as how to smell the BS when you step in it, and that great opportunity will not pass you by.

Lie #4 - "You Need to Get Lots of Likes on Facebook and Tweet Every Day."

People like to boast about how many likes they get on Facebook (especially when they want to sell you some new marketing scheme). In response to that, I ask, "How many sales did all those likes generate?" None, I bet.

What's the point of Facebooking and tweeting all day if there's no correlation between the time spent on social media and the new sales generated? Of course, it's good to build relationships with prospects and customers, but you can't expect them magically to make their way to your website and buy something. You need a strategy in place.

Tweet Off

I don't have any patience for Twitter. In my opinion, it's a complete waste of time and energy.

For one, tweeting with your prospects all day is simply bad positioning. It shouldn't be that easy to contact you, if you want them to perceive you as valuable or busy. And, I find it entertaining to read about football players and managers getting into Twitter arguments with their followers. The last thing any high profile person needs is an app on their phone allowing any arsehole on the planet to affect their emotional state whenever THEY feel like it.

A big secret to happiness and success is to avoid all contact with negative or rude people. Important businesspeople, celebrities, authors, and artists MUST have buffers between themselves and the remainder of the negative world if they want to stay on track.

Try contacting me without paying for it, and see how far you get. You won't get to me. You can't call me, you can't email me, and you most definitely can't tweet me. If you spend your time typing out a negative forum post about me, I won't read it (though my lawyer probably will).

This is my buffer between the negative world and myself, my system for weeding out all the arseholes with whom I don't want to deal. I have no desire to debate or argue about ANYTHING with people who have no intention in giving me any money for my time.

Lie #5 – Too Many Emails Will Annoy Your Prospects – That's Spamming People!

If I had a pound for every time someone told me I send too many emails!

Before I give you the tried and tested rules for sending emails, let me share a secret with you – every time I send an email to my prospect list, I make money. Every time!

John Lennon once said, *"I'm going to sit down and write a swimming pool."* Once you've built a decent list of interested prospects, you can literally send them an EMAIL and make money any time you want.

However, there are a few important rules to follow:

1. ONLY email YOUR prospect list – the list you build up using the lead-generation strategies I present in this book. Recipients should know who you are. Build up trust with your prospects and never abuse it.

2. NEVER buy or rent an email list. I don't care how good the slick owner says the "opt-in" list is, they don't work. No one ever opts in to receive offers from anyone and everyone with something to say. It's as simple as that. If you do give in to the temptation of easy money, the ISP's will blacklist you, and then you're finished. *There is a way to buy recently opted-in lists for specific information. read my ethical spammer report later in this book.*

3. DON'T TRY TO SELL on every email, and avoid offering "discounts" or "special offers." In fact, delete those words from your vocabulary. As a rule of thumb, you can offer a product or service once out of every seven to ten emails.

4. DON'T SEND BORING NEWSLETTERS. With few exceptions, most people hate them. They would rather get a personal, informative email from you. Not another faceless, boring newsletter.

5. MAKE SURE your prospects know what they have opted in for. If you say something like, "Sign up for my free email course, 27 Things They Don't Want You to Know About Life Insurance," readers can hardly complain if you send them 27 emails (although some still still do). Once you've built up some trust and established yourself

as someone who sends good emails, they will be happy to receive more.

6. IGNORE CRITICISM and abusive emails. If someone tells you to "stop sending me these bloody emails, you stupid f***," take it as a compliment. You're completely on the right track by getting rid of the people you DON'T want as customers.

Email offers you an incredible opportunity to build and maintain a relationship with your prospects and customers. As long as you always send interesting, relevant information, people will be happy reading your emails. And when you get that part right, the more emails you send, the better.

I am a member of a number of high-end mastermind groups. One is Perry Marshall's Roundtable. Perry is the world's #1 Adwords marketing guru. Perry sends me two emails EACH DAY, and I devour every one of them.

Another great copywriter, Jon McCulloch, will ask you to sign up to his marketing tips course on his website, and then you get one email per day for life. His emails are all good, informative, interesting, funny, and controversial; I am in the habit of looking out for them in my inbox. I bought my first product from Jon after he sent me email number 87.

I send one email to my list 3-7 times per week. Yes, many people opt out, and some people still tell me to *'fuck off'*, but that's great.

Another bonus of sending daily emails is you get rid of the arseholes very quickly. If someone is prepared to tell me to *"fuck off"* after receiving a simple email, it's unlikely they were ever going to become a customer, whether I emailed them or not.

So, how many emails do you send your prospects and customers?

10,000-Year-Old Principles vs. App of the Month

Email presents an outstanding opportunity to build relationships with people in much the same way humans have done for thousands of years. The methods or tools of communication are different over time, but the principles are almost always exactly the same. If you want to make money online, you build trust with your prospects. It's not about tricking people; it's about being honest and upfront about whom you are and what you represent.

Most people think the internet requires doing something different. Nope.

The internet is just another communication tool. So, you do what has always worked. Too many businesses try to sell to visitors the moment they arrive on the website when they should be taking the opportunity to begin a relationship with these prospects. Offer free advice and prove you are the expert they need – that you can solve their problems.

If you reposition yourself as a problem-solver instead of a seller of goods and services, people will warm to you instead of your competitors. Offer valuable reports, advice, and all your best secrets for FREE. You need to PROVE you are as good as they HOPE you are.

People buy when they're ready to buy, not when you are ready to sell. The point is that if you're always in front of your prospects, you'll be there when they're ready to buy and will be the natural choice. Nothing beats building and maintaining personal relationships.

Lie #6 - You Need to Cut Your Prices to Get More Customers.

Most business owners simply haven't got a clue how to set their prices, and so they try to be the cheapest. The truth is that having the lowest price is not really an advantage, and having the highest price is not really a disadvantage. Because, price is rarely ever the main factor in selling. Most customers don't want "cheap" – they want good value, a sense of pride and peace of mind.

Business owners tend to look at what their competitors are charging and then set their prices a little bit cheaper or bang in the middle. This is a big mistake. It leaves you wide open for attack. You're failing to differentiate your business from your competitors.

Truth be told, this is a weak approach made by entrepreneurs who are too scared to increase prices and lose existing or new customers. Or they're worried about what their competitors think. I made this mistake myself plenty times in the past, but you'll never be truly successful with that mindset. A real paradigm shift is in order.

If you live by price, then you die by price. All it takes is one of your competitors to undercut you, or the tiniest downturn to wipe out your measly margins, and you're screwed!

But once you escape a price competitive environment, via positioning and good marketing, you really can "set your own price" for any product or service you offer.

THE WORST THING YOU CAN EVER DO TO GENERATE MORE MONEY IS CUT YOUR PRICES!

On the other hand, if you deal with price resistance by arguing that your services are of a higher quality, you'll still find your sales work difficult. Yes, people do want superior goods and services, but they don't necessarily want to pay premium prices for them. A lot of business owners fight this battle every day with their customers, and it's demoralising.

The secret is to switch the standards of comparison. Compare apples to oranges, and throw in the superior quality at no extra cost. Re-invent your products and services by packaging them up. Add value, bundle goods and services together, include delivery, offer warranties, tack on cast iron guarantees, throw in desirable bonuses, create payment plan options, and sell VIP membership clubs. You can always charge more for these extra services. There are other ways to mix it up as a well.

Here's a simple idea that applies to a wide range of industries. If you offer a service, throw in some products, and if you offer a product, include a service.

Here's another. If you've already set your prices for a product or service and don't want to change things, that's fine. Keep the existing offer at the current price, and design two or three premium package options, like "Gold" or "Platinum." Give your customers several choices, and they will most likely choose the middle option, as long as it's appealing enough.

This is one of the most powerful sales tactics about which I know. Which reminds me ...

The Old Tricks Still Work Best

Some of the best sales tactics have worked for thousands of years and still work today. For example, the salesman says, "This 'widget' normally costs $150, but you can have it today for just $99!"

Okay, your customers aren't stupid, and neither are you. We all see right through these simple gimmicks. But guess what? THEY STILL WORK!

We all love to think we're getting a great bargain, even if we subconsciously realise we're fooling ourselves. Then we rush home to tell everyone about it because it helps justify buying the damn thing.

"Well, Mary, it was actually priced at $150, but I got it for just $99. How bloody smart am I?"

Savvy business owners and marketers learn to change the rules of the game and set their own prices based on how much they want to make. Forget about playing fair. All your life you've been conditioned to play fair, and that subconscious conditioning is holding you back. It's time to change the rules to suit you and your business.

And guess what happens when you charge more for your services? You make more money! That's right – there's more cash to go around. That means you can spend more on marketing, hire more staff, pay better salaries, pay yourself more, and deal with less customers.

I ran teacher training courses in Koh Samui, Thailand for around ten years. It was a challenging business. It involved setting up observed teaching practices in local schools in Thailand, which required extra staff and some tricky organisation and logistics. We charged twice as much as our competitors and we got twice as many customers, who were much higher quality.

They positioned themselves as the cheapest school on the market, cramming in as many students as possible. We positioned ourselves as the highest quality course, with a limited number of available seats. They usually had 30 students, each paying around USD$1,000 per standard course (a logistical nightmare). We had around 20 students, all of them paying $2,000 for a premium package. They ran four-week courses (the industry norm), and we ran a two-week course with an online module included – a new concept in the industry.

We were different!

Sometimes we even got cheeky emails from our competitors. They told us we were "ripping off" our students by charging "too much" for a two-week, Training course.

Actually, I firmly believe THEY were the ones ripping off their students by charging less and cramming more students into the classroom. They were robbing their students of a quality learning experience. This also meant they were unable to afford good support, and they never had enough cash to invest in marketing. As a result, we made more money and enjoyed higher profits than they did.

Most of our competitors have since gone bust! Beating your competitors is all about finding or inventing an unfair advantage for yourself. Make price comparison impossible for your customers.

Make it impossible for your competitors to keep up with you. And, who cares what they think? If they're pissed off at you, you're firmly on the right path to success. If they are giving you shit, they are the ones experiencing negative emotions, and it's probably because you're winning. The more shit they give you, the happier you should be!

Lie #7 – It's Easy to Make Money Online
(Anyone Can Run This Business)

It's amazing how easily you can tell what someone's really thinking, or what they really want, by listening to what they say. You don't have to be an expert or psychologist to work this out, either.

Here's is a tip. Whenever anyone says anything at all – whether it be your wife, husband, friend, or partner – focus on two things. What they're saying... And why they're saying it.

The most common question my new clients have when they want some advice on starting a new business, marketing online, or making more money from their existing business is ..."*Jimmy, can you optimise my website for Google? I want more traffic.*"

I hear what they're saying, but what they really mean is:

"*Jimmy, can you sort out my website for me so I can just sit on my arse while Google sends me lots of traffic, bringing me lots and lots of money for doing absolutely bugger all? Also, I need to ensure that if it fails that I can blame you. Deal?*"

Here's What You Need to Know

The qualities needed to set up and run a successful online or offline business today are exactly the same qualities needed in business 15, 50, or 2,000 years ago.

Determination, persistence, burning desire, continuous self-improvement, hard work, ongoing education, testing and measuring, smart marketing, expert advice – all the same principles apply. And what it comes down to is that you need to change YOU before you can change how much you earn.

With the internet, everyone thinks they can get a piece of the action without putting in real effort. Everybody says they want to run their own business and get rich, but if you actually handed most people a ready-made, proven business template on a silver platter, they'd give you 100 excuses why the time's just not quite right for them!

Why?

Most people are scared shitless of taking on the responsibility for their own success or failure. So, when they approach me about starting a business and ask me to "take care of all that marketing stuff," they're subconsciously telling me that they want to hand over all responsibility to someone else like Google ... or ME!

At least if they fail in that type of scenario, they can conveniently pass the blame.

And if the approach succeeds? Well, who wouldn't want business success without effort? But with that approach ... anything resembling success is EXTREMELY unlikely!

Listen, I used to search for shortcuts and make excuses, too. But I discovered that you must be prepared to embark on a journey of self-discovery and self-improvement before success in your business can be fully realised.

And you simply cannot rely on others to send you customers. You can do a MUCH better job marketing your own business than ANYONE else!

Did you know that most people are actually more scared of success than they are of failure?

Why do you think people spend all their spare time on Facebook, in chat rooms, gaming, blabbing on forums, and reading pointless blogs? Well, for the same reason they watch mind-trash TV like EastEnders, Coronation Street, and the X-Factor. Reality television not only provides a way to escape from their own mundane lives but exonerates them from taking responsibility.

Don't get me wrong, some of this stuff is fun. I do like Facebook because it saves me time and makes it easier to keep in touch with all my friends and family in one place. This is crucial for an international citizen. But, good things should be taken in reasonable doses, and spending all your free time watching crap TV or loitering on social websites is the equivalent of sticking your head in the sand.

Billy Connolly, the great Scottish comedian, actor, and musician – and someone I admire greatly – was once asked by an interviewer, "Billy, as someone who came from a poor, working-class background in Glasgow, an abused child with very little education, how did you get to become so obviously very talented and hugely successful?"

"Well," he replied." I didn't get it sitting watching the fucking Des O'Connor show." (these days, that's like saying 'I didn't get it watching the X factor or reality TV shows.')

That sums it all up!

Although I believe most people are capable of creating a successful business, not everyone is prepared to do what it takes. If you spent an hour a day, every day, studying the secrets of successful marketing, how long do you think it would take before you could resign from your job?

I'd wager about six to twelve months!

But how many people are prepared to make this small sacrifice? Very few (and it's just as well – more for the rest of us!). It would be wrong for me to say it's easy to make money online, but it's fair to say that it's easier now than it ever was to start your own business ... IF, and only IF, you're prepared to commit yourself to learning! And these days you don't even have to leave the house to spend countless hours in the library in order to learn (though it's a great focus tactic).

If you want to grow a successful business, start by working on your self-image. Convince yourself that you deserve success, and then develop the confidence to take on the responsibility necessary to succeed.

Which brings me to … positive thinking!

I've read stacks of books on positive thinking, and I'll let you in on a wee secret … Most of them are CRAP!

There are two ways to approach positive thinking. First, the old-fashioned positive mindset.

You walk into a garden full of weeds, place your hands over your eyes, and proclaim, "THERE ARE NO WEEDS IN THIS GARDEN. THERE ARE NO WEEDS IN THIS GARDEN. THIS IS A BEAUTIFUL GARDEN." Anyone who has ever been involved in the multi-level marketing world of bullshit knows this one very well.

The correct way to adopt a positive attitude is to walk into the garden and say, "This garden has lots of potential. Let's deal with the weeds, haul off the junk, and landscape it – then it'll be a bloody beautiful garden."

Hey, not everything in the world is bright and shiny. It's normal and healthy to be pissed off at times, too. In fact, most of my biggest successes came after I got really angry and pissed off that things weren't going the way I wanted. This gave me the motivation to work hard and fix a problem, while always maintaining a quiet belief that said, "I WILL FIX THIS."

There's a profound difference between shouting feel-good affirmation at the mirror and having a quiet feeling of determined confidence that you will succeed in a particular project or situation.

I Just Want to Be Happy

The word "JUST" says everything about the person who utters this ridiculous statement. People who say they "just want to be happy" haven't got a bloody clue what happiness is, and they haven't figured out that you can NEVER achieve a permanent state of happiness. Which is just as well because you'd get bored with it, and then you'd be unhappy.

I don't know how many times I've heard people say things like, "If I could just win the lottery, then I'd be happy." They want to sit on their fat, lazy arses and HOPE someone just gives them £23 million quid after spending a few pounds on a lottery ticket! That's their one shot at happiness?

Like virtually all other wealthy entrepreneurs, I've worked extremely hard to create my exact level of success. That's twelve to fourteen hours per day, six or seven days a week, for the best part of ten years to make a measly USD$1 million dollars. And guess what? I've lost count of the number of months I had to pay my staff first and go without a salary!

Being "comfortable" or "happy" is a dangerous place to be because you'll stop setting goals, you'll drink more alcohol, you'll overeat, and you'll let things fall apart. And when that happens, you become fat and truly unhappy.

Tony Robbins explains this much better than I can:

Quote: ["We all have the ability to take absolute charge of our lives — but having the ability isn't the same as using it. Life is full of pitfalls that prevent us from maximizing our full potential. The 5 Keys to Wealth and Happiness is your map to where some of these pitfalls are, and your guide to overcoming them. If you master these keys, there's no limit to what you can do!

Key #1: You must learn how to handle frustration.

Frustration can kill dreams. It can change a positive attitude into a negative one, an empowering state into a crippling one. Look at almost any great success, and you'll find there's been massive frustration along the way. All successful people know to plow through roadblocks, using each setback as a learning experience.

Key #2: You must learn how to handle rejection.

Is there anything in the human language that stings more than a "no?" How often have you decided not to try for a position at your company, make a sales call, or take an audition because you didn't want to be rejected? There are no real successes without rejection. The more rejection you get, the better you are, the more you've learned, and the closer you are to your outcome.

Key #3: You must learn to handle financial pressure.

Handling financial pressure is about knowing how to get and how to give, knowing how to earn and how to save. Money is like anything else in life; you can make it work for you, or against you. Learn to deal with financial pressure with the same purpose and elegance as other things in your life, so money is no longer a source of unhappiness or compromised ideals.

Key #4: You must learn to handle complacency.

We've all seen people — celebrities, athletes, business owners, etc. — who reach a level of success and then stop. Comfort can be a disastrous emotion because when we get too comfortable, we stop growing, creating, sharing, and adding value. The key to managing complacency is to stay focused on your vision and make sure you don't "major in minor things.

Key #5: Always give more than you expect to receive.

This is the most important key because it virtually guarantees true happiness. Most people spend their time thinking about how they can receive. Our lives change the moment we change our focus from what we can get to what we can give. The key to any relationship is you have to give first and then keep on giving. Don't stop and wait to receive!" - END QUOTE] Source www.tonyrobbins.com

Money, Money, Money

Let me share a secret with you. Money does not make you happy, sad, comfortable, generous, greedy, evil, or good.

Listen up because this next part may be the best piece of money advice you EVER get in your entire life.

Money makes more of who and what you already are. Write it down and memorise it – I'm serious.

If you're a generous person, more money will make you more generous. Are you greedy? Then more money will make you greedier. Happy? More money will make you much happier. If you're evil, a pile of cash can make you more evil. If you're fat, you'll become obese; if you're sad, you'll probably become depressed; if you're moody, you'll no doubt become unbearable; and if you're someone who like a few drinks every night, chances are you'll drink yourself to ruin …

You need to change YOU before you can make lots of money.

A friend of mine who has always been overweight often tells me he would get a personal trainer if he won the lottery. No, he bloody wouldn't! He'd get a personal chef and he'd get fatter.

I pointed out that a personal trainer at the local gym costs just a few hundred pounds/dollars a month, and that he could easily afford it right now. I also mentioned that training three to four times a week (with or without the trainer), along with a small change to his daily eating habits, would solve his weight problem completely within a couple of months.

People don't like it when you tell them their problems are no one's fault but their own, but it's clear my friend. It's all about daily habits. Habits not just in what you do each day but also your thought habits, such as how you control negative and positive thoughts and feelings.

So NO, it's not "easy" to make money online and not "everyone" can run a business unless there is massive shift in their beliefs and attitudes.

Lie#8 - You Just Have to Get Your Name Out There

"Ads that win awards rarely generate sales and ads that sell rarely win awards." - Perry Marshall

There are effectively two types of advertising, "direct response" advertising and "brand" advertising (otherwise known as BS advertising).

One of the great lies of advertising is this: *"Just get your name out there and run some ads."* This lie was the key reason for the big DOT.COM crash back in 2000.

Here is a top secret tip. The ad agencies and newspaper reps don't know how to advertise! I'm serious – advertising sales reps and agencies alike haven't got a clue how to advertise effectively. Yes, they create great-looking presentations with nice images and cute headlines, but that doesn't mean they work, and when they do, it's often nothing more than luck.

See, ad agencies have an agenda. Getting you more customers and increasing your profits is not at the top of their list. Creating award-winning ads; serving the ego of the customer (you); being clever, cute, and funny; and looking good to their peers ... those things are all much more important to agency staff, whether they admit to it or not. That's the truth.

And can you blame the ad agencies for giving their customers exactly what their customers ask for? Of course not

The Solution – Direct Response Advertising

Forget about clicks, traffic, social media, activity, tweets, engagement ... and all that other bullshit. Just ask yourself this: "Are the leads converting to customers?" Yes or no? This tells you everything you need to know.

If you want to save yourself a fortune in business, remember this – all advertising MUST do one of two things: generate sales ... or generate sales leads. By holding all advertising to this standard, you can instantly tell if your campaign is working.

I'm not saying branding is never important, but your "image building" should always be a secondary goal of direct response advertising. Unless you're a big stupid corporation with more money than sense, don't go into the market trying to brand yourself to success. It's a surefire way to sink your marketing budget, and perhaps your entire company ...

Here are the 4 fundamental reasons why most advertising doesn't work:

1. No attention-grabbing headline. Using the business name and location   doesn't work as a headline. Cute and clever rarely works.
2. No USP (unique selling proposition) or stated reason(s) to choose you over competitors.
3. No compelling offer. Free report, guide, consultation, irresistible offer.
4. No call to action with a deadline. What to do next. Ask prospects to act before a specific date or it's gone.

The trick is to get people to send you their contact details in exchange for a free offer, report, guide, DVD or something irresistible.

Track and Measure Everything

If you're directing people to a website, you need to set up a special web page that also only appears in your ad. This will ensure that you can clearly identify who, if anyone, responds to your advertising.

A cheap, low-tech system for tracking *offline* advertising, on the other hand, is to list a different contact name in each offline publication and consider each a separate advertising campaign. For instance, ask readers of one magazine to "call Steve" and another to "call Mary." Make this the first thing your sales staff asks for and take note.

You have LESS than five seconds to get your visitor's attention on a website. That's five seconds to show them you've got the perfect solution to their problem. So, the first thing they should see is a headline that clearly states the biggest benefit your site has to offer.

If no one sees your headline, no one will see your ad. It's the most important element of any ad for this reason, and one small change here can increase or decrease your response rate by as much as 700%.

Everything you say in advertising must be very, very specific. A headline should talk about your customers, not about you. Remember, no one cares about YOU or YOUR company.

A headline should draw readers into the ad, but it should not attempt to be cute or clever in the style of the corporate ad agency. It should offer a benefit, provoke an emotional reaction, or just get people interested enough to read more. Do not make your company name the highlight; it's a waste of space. No one cares about YOUR company name. THEY only care about THEIR problems and how YOU can address THEM!

Good places to study ads include Yahoo or MSN home pages, tabloid magazines, and newspapers. Popular editors all admit that they spend more time choosing good headlines than they do choosing the articles on which to put the headlines. After all, if the magazine doesn't get taken off the shelf and bought in the first place, it doesn't matter how good the stories are!

Here are some powerful headline strategies to keep in mind, whether writing for newspapers, magazines, or Google Adwords:

- Promise readers the most important benefit.
- Always identify your ideal prospect.
- Announce news if possible.

The Advertising Secret Formula That Always Works

Every piece of advertising, webpage, sales letter, brochure, or banner ad you send out MUST include ALL of these ingredients:

- A powerful headline that commands attention.
- An emotionally-provocative, benefit-driven message that clearly states your USP.
- A compelling "call to action" offering something valuable for contacting you.
- A deadline, scarcity of availability, or BOTH.

Oddly enough, most advertisements don't include ANY of these ingredients; at best, there's always at least one or two bits missing. If you want to join "most advertisers" and leave all of these ingredients out of your ads too, then send your advertising budget to a good charity where it might actually do some good.

And remember, newspaper ad reps, yellow pages reps, ad agencies, and anyone who makes money selling advertising will do anything to convince you otherwise.

They don't want you to track and measure your results. After all, that's how they get paid!

Lie#9 – Build It and They Will Come

Looking for a great product to sell before researching and selecting the market is the single biggest, most fatal mistake that 90% of new entrepreneurs make.

The phrase "build it and they will come" may have been true once, but not anymore. A more accurate statement for the 21st century is, *"Build it and they will come ... as long as they know about it and have a good reason to visit you!"*

Isn't it shocking that the reason most people fail in their business is found right here at the very beginning? It's like building a house on soggy swamp mud. Hey, I've been there before. I just couldn't wait to get started, and I was deeply invested in the false belief that if the product was good enough it would sell itself.

It never did.

Find a niche market to target. You must identify a "group of people" who are <u>easy to reach</u> and actively <u>looking for a solution</u> to their problem. You MUST identify this niche and the problem before you think about what product or service you're going to sell to them.

See, most people come up with a product they ASSUME people will want and try to force it on the market, only to be left totally bewildered when no one wants to buy what they're selling. Maybe if they sold what people want to buy, instead of what they themselves want to sell, they'd have better results!

Another common marketing myth is that you just have to meet your customer's needs. Sure, there's truth in this, but here's the naked truth:

PEOPLE DON'T ALWAYS BUY WHAT THEY NEED; THEY BUY WHAT THEY WANT!

So, carefully define your target market. Never try to appeal to everyone; that's a very expensive mistake and can kill your business before it even gets off the ground. GO NICHE!

And once you do determine a profitable niche, don't just give people what they need. Instead, try to find out what people want (hint: often, just asking them goes a long way).

Case Study – The Thailand Experience

Back in 2002, I was backpacking around Asia and discovered that I'd lost ALL my money on the stock market. There I was, broke and lost in the chaos of Asia. What could I do? I had no choice but to spend a few months teaching English.

But I quickly found out that teaching was a lot of work for very little money, so I decided to up the ante and start my own teacher training program for young graduates who wanted a gap year teaching experience in Thailand. If you're not familiar with the English-learning industry, all new teachers have to complete a four-week TEFL (Teaching English as a Foreign Language) course before teaching overseas.

Of course, the market was saturated with TEFL course providers, but hey, it always seems like you've come late to the game when you come across profitable markets. I dived in anyway. I offered a TEFL training course with a job package, just like many other providers. I "thought" my customers wanted to take a TEFL course in Thailand and then land a job there – it only seemed like a natural conclusion.

But I quickly started having problems getting enough students to enrol, even though I was offering an attractive package.

To discover why, I decided to run a one-day telethon campaign. The premise was very simple. We took a day to dial up everyone in our database and asked each person the magic marketing question that so few companies ever bother to ask: *"What do you want?"*

You'd be amazed at what you can find out with these four magic words ...

Our efforts paid off, and we discovered a trend. Believe it or not, no one we called mentioned anything about taking a TEFL course at all. Not once did it even come up. Rather, they all said they wanted to "live in Thailand," "explore new cultures," and "get paid to travel the world." Of course, TEFL training courses provide a great vehicle to achieve these goals, but neither the "TEFL course" nor the "job" were part of the conversation going on inside their heads.

So, with this insight in mind, we did the obvious – we built a marketing campaign around "teaching in Thailand," "the Thailand experience," and "getting paid to travel." By not even mentioning TEFL courses or work in our ads, we increased our sales by 300% within six weeks.

The moral of the story also applies to YOUR business. DON'T GIVE THEM WHAT YOU THINK THEY WANT – GIVE THEM WHAT THEY WANT.

What you need to do is tap into the dialogue that's going on inside your prospect's head and then build your product, service, USP, and marketing campaign around that conversation.

The Next Big Gold Rush

The successful integration of online socialising and online/offline marketing in the coming years will make the difference between super successful businesses and those that struggle. Facebook will be THE next big advertising platform, just as soon as it gets its act together. It has only just recently introduced conversion tracking on its advertising platform, so it still has a long way to go.

The social media giant has an unrivalled massive audience, with detailed demographic and behavioural information on each member of its site. The potential may very well represent the gold rush of the century, and it already has Google shaking in its boots.

The problem with Facebook advertising right now is that it doesn't YET work for most businesses. Why? Well, because people still go to Google to find solutions to their problems. People visit Facebook to AVOID dealing with problems. It's an escape, and because of this, users don't like being sold to at all while playing on the site.

This attitude is changing however as FB users are beginning to accept the fact that advertising is here to stay.

In one of my previous businesses, we used our Facebook page to get our existing customers and prospects chatting with each other. It served as a good word-of-mouth tool, and our customers did much of the work for us. The irony is that 99% of the traffic on our Facebook page came from the advertising we did on Google Adwords!

So start testing Facebook ads now and get good at it. When it starts to perform, it could quickly become the world's most effective advertising platform within a few quick years. And you should be poised to pounce.

I hope you enjoyed the "9 Great lies of Digital Marketing". Make notes and please heed what I say to spare yourself of the pain and misery that comes with a failed business. Now lets see how you can get more customers to your website in part 2 of my book called "52 Ways To Get More Customers."

Part Two - 52 Ways to Get More Customers

"You will get all you want in life if you help enough other people get what they want." - Zig Ziglar

A quick word before we get started. While these 52 marketing strategies, habits, and principals aren't listed in any particular order, it's crucial that you get #1 in place before you implement any of the other 51 ideas.

Do you have to implement each and every one? Well, no ... of course not. But what if you did? All 52 have the potential to bring drastic changes to your business, and every successful business I've ever come across has dozens of marketing funnels, each bringing in at least a few new customers each month.

In contrast, the vast majority of companies – the run-of-the-mill firms – have a mere one or two funnels bringing in customers, which makes them extremely vulnerable. The most common marketing funnels on which businesses depend are cold calling (a shiver just ran down my spine), free traffic from Google, a poorly organised PPC campaign, expensive print ads, and maybe joint ventures with agents or affiliates. And, some businesses don't have any marketing funnels at all! They just open the doors every day, cross fingers, and hope.

I don't think you need me to tell you how crazy that is … You don't have to implement all of these at once to take advantage, either. Aim to focus on one per week, and a year from now, you'll have 52 new marketing strategies firmly in place. Can you honestly imagine doing this and not getting more customers or increasing your profits?

Most of these strategies won't cost you a penny, but there are some that will require a minor investment. In other cases, you can make more money by simply tweaking minor details in your business, products, services, and pricing.

Remember, in marketing, advertising costs are never an expense – as long as they're getting results. Good advertising is *always* an investment.

Let's get started, shall we?

Lesson #1 -Build Your List of Prospects & Customers

Building a list of prospects and communicating with them on regular basis is the foundation for any successful business. Nothing you EVER do will be more valuable than maintaining a list of all the people with whom your business has a relationship. Unfortunately, most businesses don't even bother.

Every time I send a simple email to my list, I make money. Back in January 2012, I sent an email offering a high-end training course for an educational organisation in which I was involved. We brought in a total of USD $263,000 in four short weeks with ONE email and two follow-ups. The prospect list of around 30,000 was built from scratch over three to four years and maintained over time.

Virtually all of the customers signed within two days of the email going out, and then it took another three to four weeks to get them through the application process and collect payment. Had this email gone out to a cold or rented list, we probably wouldn't have made a penny ...

When you have a list of interested prospects who know and trust your company, you can sell new products and services to them for many years to come. This is crucial, considering that most of the products I sell now didn't even exist two years ago. Because of my list, I can create a new product any time and I already know I have a hungry audience eager to buy.

My list also allows me to get to know my customers better by asking about problems or issues with which they need help. I can then create a product to meet their needs.

Compiling a database of prospects and customers is like pouring the foundation of a new house before you start hammering the frame together – make it your first priority, or suffer the consequences.

Lesson #2 - Position Yourself as an Expert, Not as a Salesperson

Positioning yourself as an expert in your industry, rather than just as another business selling products or services, is one of the most powerful marketing strategies you can implement.

Most business owners, from one-man shows to large corporations, are focused on the sale when they should be educating their prospects first. They jump right into their pitch.

People prefer to buy from people and entities they trust and respect. One way to educate your prospects is to offer a free report or information guide teaching them something valuable about your industry, products, or services.

What problems do they have that need solving? What annoys them about your industry? What do your competitors do badly that you do better?

Tell them about it in detail, really hammering the pain points, and then offer the solution. You'll get far more qualified, happy customers this way because you tried to help them instead of just sell to them.

Very few businesses take this approach, and that's because it takes time. But if you put in the effort and invest time and money marketing the guide instead of your products or services, your prospects will be knocking down your door to give you money.

I'm not saying this will be easy – most good things aren't, but as long as the educational resources you produce aren't complete crap, you really can't fail.

End result? You get much more respect from your customers, they're more likely to buy from you more often, and they're less likely to buy from your competitors. They will be happy to pay more money to do business with you.

We'll get into this idea and where it fits in the big scheme of things more later. For now, start writing that info guide today.

Lesson #3 - The Amazing Power of Postcards

With everyone online these days, it has never been easier to stand out from the crowd by simply taking your marketing efforts offline. And one of the best methods for doing so is to send good old-fashioned postcards through the mail to your prospect and customer lists.

In these e-based times, there's something magical about receiving a tangible item in the mail. Postcards are cheap, highly effective, and hold some BIG advantages over email.

Email messages may be free, but think about it this way...

If only 80% of your emails actually make it through spam filters, only 20% of those emails get opened, only 5% of opened messages get read, and only 2% of readers then click through to view your website, how much money are you leaving on the table?

In contrast, did you know that nearly 95% of postcards get delivered and read? Simply put, people don't throw postcards in the bin until they at least have a glance at the back.

A postcard with the right message and right offer sent to the right list becomes a license to print money. Unfortunately, most modern businesses fail to see the potential of postcard marketing, or they think their customers are too sophisticated.

Here's an idea.

How about using the postcard strategy to offer your prospects the free info guide we discussed in my last lesson? In one simple communication, you can invite prospects to visit your website and download your free guide in exchange for their name and other details.

Lesson #4 - Offer a Strong Money-Back Guarantee

Offering a strong money-back guarantee can instantly increase your sales without costing you one extra dime in advertising. Many business owners are too scared to do this because they think they'll get ripped off. Sure, some people will probably take advantage of you, but if you just doubled your sales, what's the cost of a couple of refunds? Don't let your dented ego get in the way of making profits!

Every time a customer purchases your product or service, they're taking a risk. And that's often what holds them back. In order for that resistance to disappear, they need to be sure you'll deliver on time, for starters. And then that you will fix any problems promptly if something goes wrong.

But why should the customer take all the risk when YOU can remove this barrier to entry completely by assuming the risk yourself? Offering a strong money-back guarantee, without any tricky small print, will massively increase your conversions. This is a fact. And if you think about it, the customer will likely get his/her money back anyways if you deliver a poor product or service, so you may as well be up front about it at the beginning and reap the conversion rewards.

When Domino's Pizza got its start, for example, it entered an extremely crowded marketplace. But, within a few years, it quickly became the number one pizza company in the USA. How? The company had identified a serious flaw with all other pizza companies. Back in the day, when you wanted a pizza delivered, it arrived whenever the driver bothered to turn up, and that meant it was usually cold by the time you dug your teeth in.

The Domino's guarantee became its USP and a marketing legend in its own right: "Fresh, Hot Pizza Delivered to Your Door in 30 Minutes or Less, Guaranteed." How many free pizzas did it give away? Plenty. But a better question is how many did it sell?

Far more than its competitors...

This guarantee is now common in the pizza world, but Domino's was the first to offer it; and, as a result, the company became the market leader in many countries. It's important to note that the pizzas weren't that much different from those being served by any other pizza company.

It built its success on a strong USP and a money-back guarantee.

Lesson #5 - Sell to Existing Customers

I think you'll agree the biggest headache you have is always trying to find new customers without paying through the nose. After all, that's why you're reading this book! If you're like most business owners, you may be overlooking the most reliable resource out there for new sales, and it's sitting right under your nose...

Existing customers!

Call your existing customers right now, or send a letter by FedEx. Ask them how they're doing. Find out if they're having any problems with which they need some help . I can almost guarantee you'll get repeat business.

Recognising this reality, you should constantly be creating new products and services to offer to your existing customers. Don't worry about pestering them. They'll be subconsciously pleased you're thinking about them, and they expect you to keep in touch anyways.

Why is this so effective? Well, existing customers are much easier to sell to than some stranger who doesn't know your company, and because it doesn't cost you much to make a phone call, you really have nothing to lose.

A word of caution, though: if you haven't contacted them for a while, DON'T email them at this stage. This is a sure way to alienate your audience. You can send an email as a follow-up to a call or letter, but don't send any new offers this way unless the move is part of a carefully thought-out strategy.

Most customers unsubscribe or go elsewhere because they don't feel valued and respected. Bear this in mind with any offer you make. Don't send "20% off" offers out of the blue. People hate this kind of advertising, and it totally undermines your value and positioning; not to mention there's a much better way to make discount offers, which I'll cover later in this series.

First, though, how about a magic secret on how to sell repeatedly to existing customers…twelve to sixty times or more?

Lesson #6 - Create Recurring Products & Services

This one's a real game-changer. Any business with a recurring product or service and a fairly high retention rate is bound to become a mind-blowing success.

Remember what I said about selling to existing customers? Well, what better way to do so than with a recurring product that locks in a sale from existing customers each and every month, automatically!

There are dozens of ways to do this. Warranties, memberships, clubs, support, subscriptions, and websites all come to mind. You need to invent something that adds on to your business without changing your entire model.

Here's an idea. By the time you finish this book, you'll already be a marketing expert, at least compared to everyone else in your industry. Why not apply these principles and strategies into your business and then go on to teach others in your industry all the secrets for a monthly membership fee?

You could also just expand on your current offerings by mixing things up. If you offer a product, for instance, add a service. If you offer a service, add a product.

Start thinking about how to get your customers committed to an automated monthly payment plan or an exclusive membership club in exchange for substantial discounts and cool benefits.

This is what separates the highly-successful business from the ones struggling at the back of the pack.

Lesson #7 - Raise Your Prices; Crush Your Competitors

"Why do people say 'grow some balls'? Balls are weak and sensitive! If you really wanna get tough, grow a vagina! Those things take a pounding." --Betty White

Believe it or not, raising your prices can easily increase your profits by up to 500% or more! Assuming you've got the balls, or even better, the vagina! It doesn't cost you a penny, and in many cases, you won't lose a single customer.

Most business owners are scared shitless at the thought of raising prices, even though every single one of them wants to. They're too afraid they might lose customers or be perceived as greedy by their peers.

Think about it this way. It's your responsibility to offer a higher value service to your customers and charge as much as you're worth. This is the best way to protect the survival of your business for you, your family, and your employees. You owe it to yourself and those around you to keep your business alive and to make it grow! And you owe it to your customers to help them get the highest-value service possible.

How can you implement this without losing a single customer?

The easiest approach to raising prices is to add new "packages" for your products and services. For example, you can introduce three new package choices: Silver, Gold and Platinum. Whatever you're selling now becomes "Silver," and then you expand on that to create a more expensive "Gold package" and an even more expensive "Platinum package."

If you offer a product, add a service. If you offer a service, add a product. That's it!

And guess what? If you sell a $100 product with a 30% mark-up and increase your prices by $30, then congratulations, you've just doubled your profits!

If you're struggling to figure out the maths here, ask your spouse, partner, or valued employee to bend YOU over the nearest desk and give you a right good kick up the butt.

Lesson #8 – The Power of Direct Mail

"The aim of marketing is to know and understand the customer so well, the product or service fits him and sells itself." - Peter Drucker

Direct mail is the best form of marketing ever designed. Hands down.

As long as you have a good list of interested prospects and/or buyers, nothing beats sending them a personalised letter by post, which has a much higher chance of getting to the intended customer, and being read, than email ever will!

Not to mention that he or she can sit down, undisturbed, and absorb your content free of distraction.

People read emails the same way they read newspapers. Think about the last time you read the news. I'd wager that you can't remember what you read two days ago in the newspaper or in an email, but you probably remember books you read months or even years ago.

Don't get me wrong – email marketing definitely has its place. In fact, I get most of my customers through a combination of email marketing and most of the 52 other strategies mentioned in this book. But you get the point.

The problem with direct mail is that it costs a lot more money. This is the stumbling block for a lot of would-be direct marketers, who use it as an excuse to half-ass their first campaign. Most business owners tell me that they "tried it once, but it didn't work." That's not the way. Like all good marketing, you have to test a small campaign first.

You find something that works and then you tweak from there. Don't re-mortgage your house in a bid to mail the whole country until you find out what list, message, and offer gets the best results – but don't give up right out of the gate either.

Here are some areas where most people go wrong with direct mail:

- Poor quality list, wrong target market, or both.
- Not testing different mail pieces.
- Wrong message or poor content in the letter.
- No compelling offer.
- No proof.
- No call-to-action.
- No clear instructions for the prospect to follow.
- No deadline.
- No follow up with a 2nd, 3rd, 7th, or 32nd mailing.
- No tracking and measuring results.

There's a lot more time, planning, and investment required to run a successful direct mail campaign and it's certainly not as easy as it looks. True. But if you get these ten points above right, you're well on your way to a winner.

Lesson #9 - The Secrets of Email Marketing

"Whenever you find yourself on the side of the majority, it is time to pause and reflect." - Mark Twain

Just in case you're wondering, I am not going to teach you to start spamming people. Many small businesses have a knee-jerk reaction when I put the idea of email communications on the table because of all the no-class marketers who give it a bad rap. But email marketing done right is one of the best tools ever invented for keeping in touch with your prospects and customers.

It's convenient, it's free, and your messages are delivered instantly.

However, most businesses, PR companies, and ad agencies don't have a clue how to use this communication medium properly.

Here's an example. Most "experts" tell you that you "can't send too many emails, or you'll annoy people." Your business peers have probably already warned you that "no one buys from an email."

Bullshit!

I send an email virtually EVERY SINGLE DAY to my list. The only time I miss a day is if I get bogged down traveling or am unravelling a family crisis. And EVERY time I send an email, people buy something and I make money. End of story.

The secret to getting this right is to make sure your emails are interesting and relevant. It's also imperative (legally so) to get permission from your prospects before you email them…and I DON'T mean by tricking them into *not* ticking the "don't email me" box.

Setting expectations is another key to success, so make it 100% clear what they will get, too. As long as you're relevant, interesting, and *not* boring, people will be happy to receive your daily emails and read them. Considering that most people are content to sit and read a newspaper each day, or pore through pages upon pages of a book, why would they not be excited to receive vital, interesting information on a regular basis about a topic that intrigues them?

Don't believe this will ever work? Not so fast – I got permission from you to send emails, didn't I? How did I do it? By offering you my free 52-step marketing course, you already know up-front that you'll be receiving one email per day for 52 days, and as long as you find these emails informative and NOT BORING, you'll be happy to get every single one.

Sure, you probably won't have time to read them all, but you'll certainly read as many as you can. And because they arrive on a daily basis, you're bound to start opening them sooner or later. You can opt out any time you want, which means you're always in control.

Quick confession – I do still get complaints from people now and again telling me to *"fuck off and stop sending me emails."* But who cares? I'm not spamming these people – they opted in, just like you did, and it's hardly my fault they forgot. For all I know, they're schizophrenic and one of their other personalities signed up.

In any case, I don't lose a minute's sleep over it. I'm delighted when people tell me to *"fuck off"* because it means I just got rid of someone I DON'T ever want as my customer. I'm weeding out the crazies, the assholes, the time-wasters, and the tyre kickers – and hey, that's fine by me.

Besides, I get far more people emailing to say "thanks." One more thing: Don't EVER buy or rent email lists. No one EVER opts in to receive emails knowing that anyone and everyone will have free reign to send then just about anything they want, so the quality of email lists for sale is always very, very poor. If you've set the standard for a trusted relationship, however, and you've properly set expectations, emailing your list every day keeps the relationship alive and sets the stage for a golden marketing opportunity.

Lesson #10 - Don't Listen to the Guy Down at the Local Pub

"Everyone's got a butt and a point of view." - Hank Williams Jr (from the song 'That Ain't Good')

If you asked me to recommend ONE single way to increase your profits and eliminate stress, at no extra cost, I would tell you this – stop taking advice from the wrong people! People who offer advice freely may mean well, but that doesn't make them any more qualified. And like it or not, taking advice from mediocre people is a sure path to mediocre profits.

Just look around you. It doesn't take a genius to see that the vast majority of people have zero clue about money and success. That's why 95% of people retire broke. These punters at the pub are the same ones who will tell you "success is based on luck" and that "money isn't important." Ha! Try buying a beer without money and see what happens.

It's all bullshit!

If you were in the company of self-made millionaires, what advice do you think they'd give you? I've yet to meet one self-made millionaire who believes "success is built on luck." In fact, compare the total number of failures they (and I) have had in business, and life in general, against the number of successes they've had, and you'd probably be more accurate thinking they were are ALL A BUNCH OF UNLUCKY BASTARDS!

In my mastermind circles, I'm surrounded by highly successful, extremely wealthy people. If I need some business or marketing advice, who do you think I turn to? My well-intentioned family? The guys down at the pub? Or my mastermind group of experienced business people?

If you wanted to build an airline company from the ground up, to whom should you speak? Richard Branson or your brother-in-law, the plumber? I bet your brother-in-law has plenty of opinions on the matter. But opinions and bums have a lot in common; everyone has one, and they're usually full of shite!

Start hanging out with happy, healthy, wealthy people and you'll eventually become one of them.

Lesson #11 - How to Generate Referrals & Word-of-Mouth Advertising

This is another underused goldmine that can deliver more customers and more sales for virtually zero investment. Word-of-mouth recommendations are far more powerful than the best advertising or marketing in the world – because what someone else says about your business is far more powerful than anything you have to say.

If you implement all 52 to these marketing tips, people will rant about your company on their own, but there are a number of things you can do to get the good gossip really going.

4 Tips for Turbo-Charging Your Word-of-Mouth Marketing

1. Just Ask! Ask every happy customer if he/she has friends who might benefit from your products or services.

2. Maintain the utmost integrity. Offer a great service, fix problems without delay, and offer refunds promptly.

3. After-the-Sale Gifts. Send genuine gifts to your customers after a sale, with no obligation. How many businesses do this? I can only remember one merchant in the last 20 years ever sending me a sincere, no-string-attached gift. Don't let the lack of companies using this method fool you after all, 20 years is a long time for one sale to stick in my mind.

4. Over-Deliver. Always give a bit extra to every customer. A wee thoughtful touch goes a long way. For example, my wife and I popped into a new Italian restaurant a few years ago in Bangkok, and I ordered a glass of red wine while chatting with the owner. The waitress brought over a glass of white wine by mistake (a common mistake in Thailand, even though I speak Thai). When the owner realised what had happened, he quickly apologised and offered to bring me what I asked for. "No, that's alright," I said. "Either red or white will do; I'm happy to drink it." "Great, it's on the house then.." he insisted.

A small but really nice gesture, and this type of thing does not go unnoticed. In fact, I'm now telling you and over 300,000 people about it – how's that for word-of-mouth?

Unfortunately, I can't remember his name or the name of the restaurant. If only he'd have taken down my details and emailed me invitations, VIP member cards, 2- for- 1 meal vouchers, flowers for my wife, and so on and so on ...

Are you starting to see the big picture here?

Lesson #12 -Up sell Every Customer

You've probably never thought about it this way, but you OWE it to your customers to offer an up-sell. I know, I know - you're worried you might annoy them or come across too pushy. Nothing could be further from the truth.

See, whether you know it or not, your attitudes and beliefs have been influenced by your upbringing. Your cultural conditioning keeps you from "asking for too much" or "being greedy." It's a difficult to overcome these barriers we put up inside our minds, but it is possible to maximise every sale without annoying your customers or putting on the hard sell.

Professional selling is about solving problems for your customers by offering solutions. If someone buys a camera, is there any harm in asking if they want a tripod or a protective carry case? And what about a lifetime damage/ theft insurance plan or warranty? Aren't you doing them a *disservice* by not asking?

Get this – all you have to do is ask and 20% of your customers will buy the up-sell. This is virtually guaranteed if you structure it correctly. Why?

Because they want it. Hell, they very well may even need it. So, try it. Once again, if you sell a product, offer a service. If you sell a service, then offer a product. Just ask. EVERY time. And watch your profits soar.

Lesson #13 - Boost Sales with Telemarketing

If there's one thing I've hated my whole life, it's cold calling.

I started my career in sales at 18, selling dusters, clothes pegs, and ironing board covers door-to-door while fighting the freezing cold Scottish wind and rain. I made a lot of money for an 18-year-old in those times, and I learnt a lot about people, selling, and myself – not to mention what it's like to depend on that next sale just to eat!

Learning experience or not, it was soul-destroying work. I finally ended up moving inside, selling various things, including advertising space, over the phone. You'd think that sitting behind a desk in a nice warm office would be far preferable to trekking through the cold wind and rain to have doors slammed in your face. Well, kind of. It is for a while, but it still ends up destroying your soul.

Cold calling is cold calling, and you want to avoid cold calling like the plague because it's one of the most demeaning things you can do, no matter how much money it puts in your accounts.

Telemarketing should never be served cold, and it should never annoy the people you're calling. Why in the world would you want to annoy potential customers?! On the other hand, the phone is a fantastic tool for following up on web form submissions or direct mail pieces. People prefer to buy from people, so making that personal connection WILL boost your sales and profits substantially.

Start by calling your existing customers. Ask how they're doing and whether they have any problems they need solving. Don't call and say, "I'm just trying to drum up some business." I bloody hate when people say that. No one cares about you and your business – they care about their problems, not yours. Not to mention, it's bad positioning and makes you look desperate.

Instead, start calling prospects and existing customers for a quick chat. And don't forget to ask for the order at the end of the call. Just ask!

Lesson #14 - Set Up Joint Ventures with Your Competitors

To be honest, this is something I haven't done much of over the years. I guess it's because I tend to be a competitive guy, and I've always considered competitors my "enemies," so I just never really wanted to connect with them.

Years back, however, I did set up one joint venture with a training company that was training teachers on Koh Samui, a beautiful island in the Gulf of Thailand. It was all one-way traffic; I was sending them all of their customers, but they weren't sending me any. To make matters worse, the owner started begrudging my 30%. At one point, she even said, "I'm giving you $500 of the $1,500 fee, which is a bit steep – can we not re-negotiate?"

Of course, I reminded her that she wasn't giving me ANYTHING, and that I was giving her $1,000 worth of business that she would otherwise not be getting! She didn't quite agree, so I quickly stopped sending her customers and began running my own courses, with my own staff.

Joint ventures shouldn't be ignored completely; a healthy arrangement can be lucrative as long as everyone benefits from the arrangement.

Another lesson to be learned from my story is the risk of relying on one joint venture for the majority of your customers. This puts you in a very vulnerable position. You could wake up one day to find your associate has changed his or her mind, and you're out of business.. just like that.

So, how do you go about finding good candidates for these types of partnerships? First, you want to avoid the mistake a lot of business owners make in trying to set up joint ventures by sending out an email blast to anyone and everyone who comes to mind. Although this can work, it's essentially cold prospecting and should be avoided.

Instead, identify your ten best candidates, call to find out who's in charge, and send a personal FedEx letter to them breaking down your offer. Follow up with a phone call, and then maybe an email.

If you don't get an answer, try another follow-up letter and another call until you get a yes or a no.

Lesson #15 - Create a Herd of Pro Affiliates

Affiliate programs offer a convenient way to tap into a new market or launch a new business with little or no cost. Instead of spending time on product creation, you can promote someone else's products and services to test the market without all the costs and risks of starting from scratch. Just be careful because many of these programs are a complete waste of time or deliver sub-par product.

On the other side of the coin, what if you're already running a business and want to set up a team of affiliates promoting your current products? Let me share the number one secret to my own success setting up and running an affiliate network. Offer a very generous commission.

That's it. And by generous, I mean that I offer a full 30-50% per sale.

I already know what you're thinking. "Wait – that's way too much! I can't afford that!" But let me explain why I do this and why you should, too.

It bloody works! If I offer a 10% commission, I'm no different than anyone else. It just doesn't motivate people enough; 30-40% is outrageous, sure, and that's EXACTLY why it works! You need to be outrageous if you want to stand out from the crowd.

And here's the thing. A 30% commission compared to 10% isn't a just 20% increase for your sellers – it's a whopping 200% more! Trust me, there are thousands of smart affiliate marketers out there who understand this perfectly well.

Who wouldn't want a piece of that action?

Listen, if you can't afford to pay out 30-40% commissions, it's most likely because you're not charging enough for your products and services. And if you really, honestly can't raise your prices more, in virtually all cases you can (there are a few exceptions) create new products/ services, packages, memberships, and warranties. If you can even just increase the lifetime value of each customer, wouldn't it be worth paying out the 40%?

You will need an automated affiliate management system

– it would be a nightmare trying to manage this type of operation without one. And it takes a bit of work and effort to establish it. But, the rewards are more than worth it.

Good affiliates can bring in heaps of customers whom you would otherwise never find.

Lesson #16 - Send Press Releases and Get Free PR

Why pay for advertising when you can get it for free? This isn't the easiest marketing job you'll ever take on, and it requires a fair degree of determination and persistence, BUT customers listen to and believe just about anything they read about you in the media as long as it's not coming from you directly.

A newspaper interview can generate thousands of dollars of free advertising, and it's much more effective than any paid advertising or advertorial in which you'll ever invest (side note: advertorials are still much better than paid ads).

Imagine you've created a free information guide about the problems customers experience in your industry, as well as the cowboys to watch carefully (don't mention any names).

And now you're trying to figure out the best way to market this guide. Send a press release to local newspapers, radio stations, and TV shows. Offer your free guide and volunteer time to talk about these issues.

Notice that we're not talking about your products or services here. We're talking about information your audience needs to know.

Look, most press releases that media companies receive on a daily basis are crap – boring, useless drivel you wouldn't wish upon your worst enemy. If you want to stand out from the crowd, hand them relevant, interesting things to talk about; and, believe me, they'll leap at the chance to put it in front of their readers or viewers.

Your first challenge is to get the thing read. As usual, send it by FedEx special delivery instead of regular post.

Note: If there's a whiny voice in the back of your mind right now, begging you to send it as an easy email attachment instead, then please go back to the beginning of this course and start reading again from scratch.

Remember, everyone else in this world is lazy. Everyone. So are you, and so am I. That's why just a little bit of effort to do things just a little bit better than everyone else goes such a long way. Go the extra mile, and you'll always come out on top.

Make sure to send follow-ups, and place a call to see if they received it. Keep persevering – it may take some tweaking to get the approach right, but you'll get there. And once you do get some PR exposure, copy the newspaper piece or radio/TV show and send it to all your customers and prospects. Bingo!

Lesson #17 – Turn Your Website Into a Direct-Response Machine

Does your website read like an online brochure? One of the best ways to get more customers and sales is to simply re-organise and turn it into a direct-response machine. My Inner Circle members have implemented this strategy for amazing results.

Believe it or not, most web designers are useless at creating a website that works. They're great at designs, of course – glorious and flashy digital concepts that impress their peers. But that doesn't mean they know anything about marketing.

Years ago, I learned this the hard way. At the time, I owned this really basic, ugly website. It wasn't much to look at, but it was making around £5,000 per month, paying all my bills, and putting food on the table. Not too shabby.

One day, I decided it was time to invest in a "more professional-looking website." I was ready for the big leagues. So, I hired a web design company in the UK. It created a beautiful site, and working with the people there was a genuine pleasure.

But my sales plummeted.

What could I do? After a few agonising weeks, I changed back to my original, boring website. Sure enough, within a few days, leads and sales started coming back in again.

Why did this happen?

It's simple, really. It was because I already had a direct-response website that was working just fine. Direct response means my site was organised to capture names and email addresses by offering a free guide, and the offer was backed up with an automated follow-up email campaign. It was jam-packed with useful information and building trust with my prospects on auto-pilot, constantly reminding them who I was.

"If it ain't broke, don't fix it," as they say.

When you build this type of trust with your audience, they're no longer price shoppers. Most people don't want cheap, whether they know it or not. They want good value, reassurance, and the security that comes with buying from people they trust.

The majority of web designers haven't got a clue how to make a direct-response website or generate money online. Bear that in mind.

Your landing page should have a number of elements that are focused on one goal, and one goal only! What's the goal: To ask every one of your visitors to exchange their details for a free information guide or short report.

The info guide will talk about their problems instead of ranting on and on about your products and services. It's an opportunity to build trust, and you expand on that trust with regular emails, proving to your prospects that you are the expert in your field and have their best interests in mind.

The elements for good direct-response marketing are:

1. Great headline and sub-headline infused with your USP (Unique Selling Position).

2. A video of you talking about your prospects' problems.
3. Opt-in box offering a free report or guide.
4. Bullet-list of benefits and some written content.

Most company websites are all about the firm, its products, or its services. These things don't interest anyone. Frankly, it's boring.

Most websites also give too many options to choose from. Banners, links, boxes, "click here," "click there"... The attention span of your average visitor is much smaller than it was even a few years ago, and people are accustomed to simple apps and search engines where they can find what they want as quickly and as easily as possible.

You must provide the same type of experience.

There is a belief amongst business owners that this approach will stop prospects from seeing their products/ services. Again, people don't give a shit about your products or services. Really! They only care about their problems and what's in it for THEM.

Are they going to get ripped off? Are you going to waste their time? Can you deliver what they need? When they need it? Why should they listen to you over everyone else out there?

All the great marketing in the world is wasted if your prospects are not being converted into leads and customers. Apply some focus in learning these principles and you stand to create a massive profit-booster for your business. Because

I'd wager that 99% of your competitors are not asking themselves these questions.

Lesson #18 - Native Advertising

Native advertising is a type of online content. It's very similar to a traditional advertorial, which is a paid placement attempting to look like an article. A native ad, however, tends to be a lot less obvious than your typical advertorial.

My experience here is minimal, but this concept could be huge, and I'm currently testing a number of native ads to gauge potential. Early results look very promising.

There's a big push on native ads right now because publishers, newspapers, and online news sites are simply not making enough money from banner ads, which have a very low click-through-rate. In comparison, native advertising has an incredibly high click-through-rate, and the level of engagement is through the roof!

People like reading this type of content because the information is usually relevant to whatever the reader is interested in at that specific moment. It's really a genius idea if you think about it. The web owner makes money, and the business owner – that's you! – makes more sales. A win/win situation.

It's easy to get it in your head that advertising will pay off simply because it's advertising. After all, if it didn't work, people wouldn't pay so much money for it, right? But people don't really trust ads – on an instinctual level, you know that already. Because YOU don't trust ads.

If you practice education-based marketing, on the other hand, you build trust and respect with your prospects. Remember Lesson #1 – it's not about just trying to sell them something.

Check out Buzzfeed or Outbrain to see how this Native Ad concept works. I'm excited, and you should be, too!

Lesson #19 - Lose Some Weight

I take it you're not easily offended? If you are, I have no clue what possessed you to read this far. And in any case, I make no apology for the shock tactics. Anyways, my mate Billy is a fat bastard! *(lovely guy, but fat all the same)*. This fact is easy for me to spot, but it's not so easy for Billy.

And he's not the only one, either. Just today I convinced myself that I'm NOT getting fat. But how can I know for sure? Am I just fooling myself?

Bear with me; there is a point here.

Have you ever noticed you were putting on some weight and worried whether you too were joining the Fat Bastards fraternity? Then what'd you do? I bet you stopped and took a real good look at yourself in the mirror. And I bet if you were honest with yourself, you'd admit that you held in your stomach and straightened your posture a tad.

You may not have even noticed, but you probably drew in your cheeks and pouted your lips, making a funny face … A peculiar attempt to make yourself look more attractive.

This is your lizard brain trying to convince you that "You look just fine, so go out and eat a big cheeseburger and fries. Oh, and treat yourself to a curry at 10pm on a Saturday night. Then sit on your arse – you deserve it!"

You'll just have to breathe in a bit harder next week, right? A week or so ago, my wife filmed me playing with the kids. I was horrified to see the guy who showed up on the screen. According to the mirror, I looked fine; but when playing with the kids, I had let my belly relax and the camera couldn't lie. I'd been caught off guard, and there was no denying how fat I'd gotten.

This is basic human psychology here; we SEE WHAT WE WANT TO SEE. It protects our little egos. We do it in our businesses, in our personal relationships, in our marketing, and, of course, when we're looking in the mirror.

I was watching a program on television in the UK a while back – I think it was a show called "Dispatches" – where these Fat SOBs were claiming that they didn't know why they couldn't lose weight. After all, they only ate healthy foods and hardly ever drank alcohol.

They insisted it was their metabolism. The poor "victims." So, the editors placed a hidden camera in the house. Indeed, both she and her big fat husband appeared to be eating nice healthy salads at home for dinner... washed down with six or seven beers (EVERY night).

The producers even followed the fat wife to her job, where she worked as a street cleaner. There she was, stuffing her face with a kebab at lunchtime, greedily helping herself to numerous afternoon snacks, and gulping down a large helping of fish and chips on the way home.

All before settling down to a healthy evening salad, of course...

Metabolism. My Arse!

We humans fool ourselves day in and day out. Your lizard brain just wants you to be comfortable, so it's hard to hate the little fella. But you need to step out of your comfort zone to challenge your beliefs and change your daily habits.

Have you noticed, for instance, how many fat bastards go to the gym or spend time sprawled out in the sauna? They only go to give themselves an excuse to eat more. Few people ever lose weight just by going to the gym or sitting in the bloody sauna (unless it's a boxing gym, perhaps).

So, what the hell has this got to do with marketing and getting more customers, I hear you ask? Well, these same principles apply to your business and your wealth. You need to challenge your beliefs and change your habits in order to grow personally AND to grow your business.

When I teach business owners how to change their marketing habits, or tell them how to improve their websites, they invariably make excuses like, "This won't work in my business," or "I don't have the time." And if they really believe that, well, then that's just the way it is.

See, what you focus on expands. If you focus on your marketing, it improves and you make more money. If you focus on your problems, then the problems become bigger. Most people focus on the wrong things, and they therefore get the wrong results.

If you want to improve your wealth, improve your health first. Exercise should be the first thing you do each morning, and try to make a habit of NOT eating fat bastard carbs and sugary stuff.

It comes down to a focus on productive daily habits, and most importantly, thought habits. Look, I'm not making this crap up. Here's what Mahatma Gandhi had to say about the subject: "*Your beliefs become your thoughts, Your thoughts become your words, Your words become your actions, Your actions become your habits, Your habits become your values, Your values become your destiny.*"

And how about this for a kick in the testicles: "*Winners make a habit of doing the things losers don't want to do.*" — *Lucas Remmerswaal*

Bad habits create bad luck...and FAT people. I rest my case.

Lesson #20 - Copy the 21 Things Rich People Do Every Day

As we've just discussed, ALL the best marketing strategies in the world won't make the slightest bit of difference for your wealth or happiness if you don't change your attitudes, beliefs, and habits. And, there's a profound difference in the way rich people and poor people think and behave.

By the way, I'm not saying poor people are all bad. Not at all; they're just poor. I was poor myself for most of my life.

Wealthy people ain't all bad either, although that's what we're conditioned to believe since childhood.

But poor people ARE always wrong when it comes to money and wealth! After all, that's why they're skint!

So, what is it that the rich do every day that the poor don't do? Tom Corley outlines a few of the differences on his website, Richhabits.net:

1. 70% of wealthy eat less than 300 junk food calories per day. 97% of poor people eat more than 300 junk food calories per day.
2. 23% of wealthy gamble. 52% of poor people gamble.
3. 80% of wealthy are focused on accomplishing some single goal. Only 12% of the poor do this.
4. 76% of wealthy exercise aerobically 4 days a week. 23% of poor do this.

5. 63% of wealthy listen to audio books during commute to work vs. 5% for poor people.

6. 81% of wealthy maintain a to-do list vs. 19% for poor.

7. 63% of wealthy parents make their children read 2 or more non-fiction books a month vs. 3% for poor.

8. 70% of wealthy parents make their children volunteer 10 hours or more a month vs. 3% for poor.

9. 80% of wealthy make happy birthday calls vs. 11% of poor.

10. 67% of wealthy write down their goals vs. 17% for poor.

11. 88% of wealthy read 30 minutes or more each day for education or career reasons vs 2% for poor.

12. 6% of wealthy say what's on their mind vs. 69% for poor.

13. 79% of wealthy network 5 hours or more each month vs. 16% for poor.

14. 67% of wealthy watch 1 hour or less of TV every day vs. 23% for poor

15. 6% of wealthy watch reality TV vs. 78% for poor.

16. 44% of wealthy wake up 3 hours before work starts vs. 3% for poor.

17. 74% of wealthy teach good daily success habits to their children vs. 1% for poor.

18. 84% of wealthy believe good habits create opportunity luck vs. 4% for poor.

19. 76% of wealthy believe bad habits create detrimental luck vs. 9% for poor.

20. 86% of wealthy believe in lifelong educational self-improvement vs. 5% for poor.

21. 86% of wealthy love to read vs. 26% for poor.

I'm going to add in one of my own. I don't have any statistical info to back up my claim, but I'd bet you all the bar girls in Thailand I'm right.

22. 99% of wealthy people take advice from other wealthy people. 99% of poor people take advice from other poor people.

Since I adopted new habits, my wealth and health has improved dramatically ... Almost like magic. If your business is struggling and you believe it's someone else's fault, then please understand that you're the one who has to change.

Lesson #21 - Split Test and Keep Testing

It could be argued that this is the number one strategy on this list for improving marketing, conversions, and sales. I deliberately placed this one deeper into the book because only savvy, dedicated people (like you) will get this far. There's no point in giving away the best strategies to those who can't be bothered to put in the work, or in this case, a little bit of reading.

If you're not doing so already, you ABSOLUTELY MUST split test your marketing, ads, web pages, telephone scripts, offers, pricing, packaging, and just about anything you can think of. You can even split test sales staff to see who has a higher conversion rate – I guarantee you'll learn a lesson worth money!

Appear like overkill? When you split test two landing pages on your website, or two ads/offers, there's no way to know which one will outperform the other. But one thing you absolutely DO know for sure is this – one WILL do better! And while I don't advocate spending months testing everything to death, it is vitally important to at least run three to four split tests on everything you can, and then leave the best performing versions running.

Because you NEVER know until you test.

Here's an example of an online split test I ran on a PPC campaign. Which keyword do you think got the best conversion rates for lead generation? The keyword strings were:

• teach english abroad
• teaching english abroad

You might be thinking this is some kind of trick question. After all, the only difference here is the "ing" – how in the world could there be a difference, let alone one significant enough to test? The fact is, neither you nor I have any bloody clue whether there'll be a difference or not until we test them.

So I did test them. And the conversion results were:

- teach english abroad = 12.3%.
- teaching english abroad = 16.2%

By the way, (i.e. 16.1-12.3 = 3.9), this is NOT a 3.9% difference but a whopping 31.7% improvement.

How's that? Two things about which a business owner must get really good are marketing and numbers. You can be absolutely crap at everything else and still be very, very successful if you master these two things. Here's how this particular type of problem works.

The Percent Problem:

Calculating a percentage increase from 2% to 10%.

First Step: Find the difference between the two numbers.
In this case, it's 10 - 2 = 8.
Second Step: Divide the resulting figure (8) by the original
number 8/2 = 4.
Third Step: Multiply the number you got in the second step
(4) by 100: 4*100 = 400%.

You're done! You just calculated the increase from 2% to 10%, and the answer is a percentage increase of 400%. You'd be amazed at how often the most simple website and advertising changes can result in a 400% increase in conversions … Split testing is a very powerful weapon to have in your arsenal.

Lesson #22 - The Ultimate Secret - The 80/20 Principle

"The 80/20 principle - that 80 percent of results flow from just 20 per cent of the causes - is the one true principle of highly effective people." - Richard Koch

Most people THINK they know the 80/20 principle, otherwise known as the Pareto principle (after the Italian economist who discovered it), but few really understand it intimately. I was one of the masses who thought I understood, until I read Richard Koch's book, "The 80/20 Principle."

More recently, my mentor, Perry Marshall, put out a brilliant book called "80/20 Sales & Marketing," which is a much easier read and helped to solidify my understanding. Both books are essential for all business owners and entrepreneurs.

If there were a magic bullet to success and wealth, then the 80/20 principle would probably be it. You could apply the 80/20 to your life, ditch most of the other stuff, and you'll still be well ahead of your competitors.

You've probably heard it said before that "hard work comes before success," or something along those lines. Or maybe someone told you that "Success comes before work only in the dictionary." This thinking may hold some truth, but there are plenty of arguments that say otherwise.

Here's a somewhat painful example. My grandfather worked in the steelworks in Coatbridge for 45 years. He retired broke, as 95% of people do, and he died at 74. So, if hard work breeds success, why did he and 95% of the population fail to get wealthy after working so hard for all of those years?

The answer is easy. Because most people work on the wrong things, or they treat all daily tasks and duties as equal. This is a big mistake. It's bloody HUGE!

One of the most bizarre habits many business owners have is they outsource the really important stuff they need to get done, such as marketing & accounting, and spend their time doing all the other things that SHOULD be outsourced.

You should always be handling the most high-value work in your organisation. Are you doing $10 an hour work, $100 an hour work, or $1,000 an hour work?

For instance, checking emails, updating Facebook, answering your phone, and dealing with petty staff issues are all examples of $10 an hour tasks. Anyone could do these things. Spending time on marketing, on the other hand, is $1,000 an hour – it creates a lot of revenue over time. Sending an important email or making a phone call to a big client might be worth $10,000 if it nails the order.

The secret is to outsource and delegate the $10 an hour shit and focus on the work that makes you $1,000 an hour. This is the basis of 80/20 time management.

The beautiful thing is that 80/20 applies to everything in the Universe. It's a natural law, and you cannot change it no matter how hard you try. 80% of the population own 20% of the wealth. 20% of your advertising brings in 80% of your customers. 20% of your customers bring in 80% of your profits. 20% of your bad customers take up 80% of your time.

Some things in your life may be 90/10 or 70/30 at times, but very rarely is anything 60/40 or 50/50.

In online marketing, it's actually more like 95/5.

A critical mistake business owners make is they look at averages. But when you recognise that the world works on 80/20, you see that the natural laws of business do not care about averages.

Big doors swing on small hinges. Identify the 20%, the most important things you need to focus on each day, and leave the other stuff to others. Write down all your daily tasks and ask yourself, which tasks can be outsourced to someone else?

Marketing and accounts are up there in the 20% of the 20%. Meetings, emails, admin, Facebook, and spending time at your mother-in-law's house ... are not!

Which 20% of your customers are the most profitable? Or could be the most profitable? Which 20% of your products are the most profitable? Or could be the most profitable? Identify and focus on the 20% and ditch the rest.

Hire a housekeeper and/or a nanny, and spend quality time with your kids instead of "because you have to" time. Get a secretary or PA, and let him/her handle emails so you can avoid the time-wasters. They can also conduct research into new projects for you and perform whatever other minor tasks you feel comfortable delegating.

Lesson #23 - Fire Bad Customers

Maybe getting rid of a customer doesn't seem like the best way to get customers, but think of it this way – the more energy and time you free up from those that rob you of both, the more you have to spread around.

According to the 80/20 principle, 20% of your bad customers take up 80% of your time … and most likely you know this to be true from experience in the trenches. So get rid of them! If they're taking up too much of your time, or being rude and disrespectful to you or your staff, FIRE THEM.

Most business owners are too scared to acknowledge that some customers aren't worth the trouble because they worry they'll be unable to replace the revenue. In my experience, and the experience of all other wealthy business owners with whom I hang out, new and better customers will always show up, especially if you get your marketing sorted.

Letting them go doesn't mean you have to be rude to them; it's always a good idea to let them go quietly. Just explain that you're no longer able to serve their needs and that it's in everyone's interests that you both shake hands and walk away.

If they won't accept it, then tell them to bugger off!

Lesson #24 - Spend MORE Money on Marketing, NOT Less

Some of the most ridiculous statements business owners make include, *"This is my marketing budget for the year,"* and, *"We've already spent our marketing budget for the year."*

This tells me three things:

The business owner hasn't got a clue about marketing.

The business owner has no idea from where his customers are coming. The business owner hasn't got a clue how much it actually costs to buy a customer!

If you knew with 100% certainty that for every £100 you spent on any form of advertising, you'd get back £150 or £200 in profits, why would you want to put a limit on this? Why would you NOT want to spend as much as possible and keep spending? Because you don't know for sure where your customers are coming from, that's why.

The four fundamental questions you need to ask yourself are:

1.Where are my customers coming from?
2.How much do I need to spend in advertising to get one customer?
3.What is the lifetime value of my average customer?
4.Which customers, products and services are the most profitable?
5.There isn't a better, more lucrative way to spend your time.

Lesson #25 - Practice Positive Thoughts & Feelings

"Everyone can rise above their circumstances and achieve success if they are dedicated and passionate about what they do." - Nelson Mandela

I first wrote this piece in an email on the 5th of December 2013, just after hearing that Nelson Mandela had died. I thought it appropriate to say a few words about Nelson Mandela and how his legacy should inspire us as business owners and entrepreneurs.

Nelson Mandela was a true freedom fighter who, despite spending 27 years in prison, never gave up and never lost hope. When he was eventually released, he never showed any signs of bitterness or resentment towards his enemies. In other words, he didn't harbour any negative emotions at all.

This was crucial to his survival in brutal conditions. How many of us get stressed and beat ourselves up over trivial business issues and events? How many people worry about their competitors or grow resentful of their successes? These are all negative thoughts and feelings that have a profound effect on your success or failure, not to mention your health.

"Resentment is like drinking poison and then hoping it will kill your enemies." - Nelson Mandela

All the brilliant marketing strategies in the world don't mean a thing if you harbour negative thoughts and feelings. Practicing positive thoughts and evoking positive feelings every minute of every day, meanwhile, will improve your health, well-being, and bank balance every time.

"As I walked out the door towards the gate that would lead me to freedom, I knew if I didn't leave my bitterness and hatred behind, I'd still be in prison." - Nelson Mandela

By the way, I'm not perfect. Sometimes I get pissed off and feel negative or resentful, just like you; but I do work hard to make sure I turn it around quickly. I'm careful about what thoughts I allow to enter my head, and I remove negative ones as soon as I notice them.

One of my favourite books, and one that made a massive difference in my life, is *Secrets of the Millionaire Mind*, by T. Harv Eker. It's a fantastic book that contains a bunch of daily affirmations about money; 95% of those who read the book won't practice them. Your competitors won't either, so if you do, you're sure to set yourself apart from the sheep. I practice them almost daily; and I promise you, it works. I doubt there are any successful people or great leaders in the world who DON'T practice daily positive affirmations, whether they realise what they're doing or not.

Nelson Mandela went from being locked in a prison cell as a convicted terrorist to the South African Official Residence for the President of the Republic of South Africa. I bet this wouldn't have happened if he had remained a bitter, resentful man who felt hard done by.

In contrast, most people spend their entire lives in such a horrible state. And then wonder why they're broke and unhappy.

The challenges of building a successful business are very real. But I would suggest your challenge in building success is much, much easier than the challenges people like Nelson Mandela faced throughout their lives! Are you ready to do what it takes?

Lesson #26 - Cancel Your Retirement You've Been Conned!

"Men do not quit playing because they grow old; they grow old because they quit playing." - Oliver Wendell Holmes

I just read a report that the retirement age in the UK is going to be increased to 69-years-old! Wow. That's a good age to retire and start enjoying your life, isn't it? Too bad for the person in his or her 50s who was banking on retirement at 65. And when the government screws up the economy again, they'll probably have to raise it to 75.

Regardless of the "official" retirement age, or whether this report is accurate or not, "retirement" is one of the biggest government cons in history. That's really the big plan? To force as many people as possible to work hard all their lives and then retire at 65 (or 69) to start enjoying themselves?

I've got two words for that plan. *Fuck.Off.*

Sometimes it really boggles my mind. I've lost count of the number of school teachers I've met who "can't wait" until they retire so they can start enjoying themselves. What the hell is all that about?

Some 95% of people who retire at 65 are broke or just have enough to get by. Most are left feeling bitter and angry about the years spent doing something they hated and dwelling on "what might have been." They're not in great physical health either, which is hardly surprising if they've been eating crap food, smoking 30 fags a day, drinking most evenings, and skipping out on the exercise for 40-odd years.

Simply put, planning for retirement creates the wrong notion about wealth, happiness, and life in general. You should not be doing a job you dislike for any longer than you need to in order to get that first bit of cash in your pocket. You should not be operating a business that's running you into the ground. You should not be slaving for 80+ hours a week with no time to spend with your family or focus on your hobbies (see my 80/20 section).

What kind of life is that? You shouldn't give up your relative youth and your valuable time for ANYONE!

And another thing, if you really loved what you do, why would you want to retire anyway? Surely you would keep going as long as your body and mind was still functioning! Of course you would.

You have to create a balance in your life. Make the most of each and every day you have on this planet. Because, sooner or later, your life will end and you probably won't see it coming.

So, don't fall for this retirement con. Instead, start building wealth by investing in your future. Invest in property, start your own business (or sell the one you have and do something else), do something that makes a difference, or start a new hobby and enjoy every minute of it.

It's never too late to do anything.

Even if you're already in your 50s, 60s or 70s – perhaps retired and/or bored shitless – get back to learning and working again. Studies have shown that those who remain active in middle to old age live much longer than those who don't, and they're much healthier and happier, too.

Move away from the dreary UK, or whatever freezing cold shithole you're living in, to somewhere like Thailand, for example, where the weather is beautiful and your money goes much, much further. Older men have a pretty good chance of finding romance with stunning 25 year old, if you think some youthful lovin' would set you straight again!

If you're an ageing woman, there's a small Island near Bali called Lombok that is secretly known as a ladies' paradise! A female friend I knew in Australia once told me about this place, and the story has since been confirmed by a number of other reliable (and very happy) female sources. What an eye opener! I'm not saying any more…

My real point is that there's a whole world of opportunity out there. Go out and explore it NOW. Stay active, enjoy life, do something you love, or start loving what you do. And to hell with retirement!

By the way, if you're not convinced and you do still aim to retire early, then remember this … retirement is a question of money, not age!

Lesson #27 - Get Better at Selling

Sales is really a "disqualification" process, not a "convincing people" process! All of the marketing steps in this book are geared toward direct-response marketing and optimisation, which means all the marketing you implement is designed to only attract qualified prospects. Your sales process needs to qualify them even further so that you only end up doing business with customers who meet your criteria.

In other words, get rid of the time-wasters and price shoppers as quickly as possible, and deal only with the healthy ones left standing. You'll save yourself a ton of time and stress.

My criteria are these:

Do they have the money? If not then I can't help them anyway, and they sure can't help me. Sure, you can make money selling old clothes at a jumble sale, but it's a much, much harder graft.

Do they lie in bed at night worrying about an immediate problem that demands to be solved? They are poised to buy today if I can meet their wants and needs.

Do they have the ability to say yes? They need to be able to say yes without asking anyone else, OR they need to have enough influence over their board to make it happen.

Do they know who I am and what I'm all about? They must have read my book or have been on my email list. My customers must respect my time and understand what I WILL do and will NOT do for them.

It's not about the hard sell, and there's really no need to sell hard if your marketing systems are in place. SUCCESS in selling is all about having the right attitude to help people solve problems. It's NOT about trying to sell people things they don't really need or want. Sorry to use an old cheesy cliché, but the definition of Success is.

S - ense of direction
U - nderstanding

C - ourage

C - ompassion

E - steem

S - elf-confidence

S - elf-acceptance

I don't use cheap tricks while I'm closing sales like, *"How would you like to pay – Mastercard or Visa?"* Or, *"Would you like the blue one or the red one?"* I prefer to just ask simple questions, such as, *"Can I go ahead and book this for you now?"*

A lot of sales advice tells you that you should avoid "Yes or No" questions during a sales close, and there's definitely a grain of truth to this. But if you've done your marketing properly, you won't need to care so much about what you say at the close. By this stage, your prospects should be biting your hand off to do business with you.

And that's how my systems work. I haven't sold anything face to face or by phone for a couple of years now. All my selling is done in sales letters, videos, DVDs, and on my website. My marketing takes care of everything by delivering qualified prospects to my order form. I only speak to clients who have, or are just about to, give me money.

That means I only do business with people with whom I want to do business. No exceptions!

This approach may not yet apply to you, and you may have a sales team you need to motivate and incentivise. But, if you focus on education marketing by positioning yourself or your company as the expert in your field, then the sales process will be fairly easy and predictable.

Train your sales staff to become problem-solvers instead of salespeople and your sales will improve massively.

Lesson #28 - Buy Gifts for Your Customers

People always talk about the next big thing and tend to overlook the opportunities right underneath their noses. Buying gifts for your customers is one of them. When was the last time you sent your customers a gift …Totally unannounced with no sales pitch or offer attached?

The power and impact of buying someone a gift is profound. Remember that old adage, "Give and you shall receive?" It's true!

Christmas offers a convenient excuse, though I prefer to send gifts at other times of the year to make a bigger impression. Send something useful or cool. Don't ever send cheap crap; it has to be TOP QUALITY.

Take the time to know your customers and send something relevant. If one of your top customers is into camping, send him or her a quality pair of binoculars or a cool new camping tool. Or how about a nice bottle of wine!

Think about it this way. If you received a really good bottle of quality wine from a company with which you did business, would you tell anyone? Or would you just keep it to yourself? I bet you would tell everyone you could think of...

It justifies your decision to do business with the company in the first place. You feel smart. You feel good about your relationship and giving money to that company. Your friends and family are probably even a little bit jealous that they never get gifts from their vendors. They want, consciously or subconsciously, a piece of the action.

The goodwill generated by this simple gesture can enhance your reputation massively, and suddenly you're getting referrals without even asking for them. Hey, I don't have a problem asking for referrals, but these are of a much superior quality.

And giving makes you feel good, too!

That is not to mention that it's so easy to go on Amazon.com these days and send just about any product that's ever been made. They do all of the hard work for you; you just make the payment.

Look, businesses don't buy things; people buy things. People are people, and they haven't changed much in the last 2,000 years or so. Send regular gifts to every customer (or at least the 20%) two to three times a year. I bet your competitors aren't doing this. Are you?

Lesson #29 - Implement a Multiple Follow Up Sequence

If there's one thing salespeople and business owners do really badly, it's following up on leads. You've got him hooked, and the next step is to reel him in. But suddenly he's gone. Where did you lose your sales lead?

To prevent this type of thing, I created a 52-step email series from my book. That gives me 52 follow-up opportunities to reach out to everyone who signs up for my email course and goes a long way to keep this from happening. Most business owners, in contrast, will follow up two or three times, and that's being generous.

Nowadays, the average person is extremely distracted. As a result, your prospects will probably need seven to fifteen follow-ups before they buy from you. Contacts could mean emails, phone calls, letters, postcards, or whatever – the more communication channels, the better!

Have a look at the number of sales we got when promoting one of my training courses in Koh Samui, Thailand. When customers came to our website, we asked them to complete an application form, and then they had to pass a telephone interview before they were accepted to attend the training course.

Email 1 = 1 Sale
Email 2 = 0 Sales
Phone Call 1 = 4 Sales
Email 3 = 2 Sales

Postcard = 3 Sales*
Email 4 = 1 Sale
Email 5 = 1 Sales
Phone Call 2 = 5 Sales
Email 6 = 2 Sales
Email 7 = 2 Sales
Final Notice Email = 5 Sales
Seminar Now Full Email = 4 Sales

Not necessarily sales directly from the postcard, but the postcard likely helped to drive all subsequent sales.

We planned to sell 25 seats, and we ended up selling 30. Not bad.

What would have happened, on the other hand, if we'd made just one phone call and sent 3 emails? Well, we would have ended up with just seven customers and left 23 on the table! How much money have you left on the table? Oh dear...

Lesson #30 - Pay Per Click Advertising

Once you've started implementing the strategies in this course, you must also take the time to study the art of getting more customers and making more sales from Google Adwords & Facebook. The same principals apply!

You cannot ignore these lucrative client sources. I have made millions from Google Adwords *(and bugger all from SEO)*, and I urge you to master these two monsters. These subjects need a whole new book, which I may or may not write later, but for now, here's a quick and easy cheat sheet for you.

People go on to Google to find a solution to a problem. People go on to Facebook to AVOID dealing with problems. So you need to approach these two platforms with a profoundly different approach.

If you want to sell to Facebook users, for instance, you need to get them OFF of Facebook and on to your website. The best way to do this is to offer a free report, guide, or something tasty like I've mentioned numerous times in this book.

Notice how these marketing principles are exactly the same no matter what marketing medium we talk about? Just because it's the internet, people assume it must be different. It is NOT different. The internet is a media platform – just like TV, email, direct mail, and the Yellow Pages.

Once you get those interested prospects onto your website, give them their freebie in exchange for their name and email address. You can then start to build a relationship with them by sending regular, interesting updates by email.

Facebook users will be comfortable with this type of marketing because you are GIVING them something and not trying to sell them anything. Those searching on Google will also appreciate a problem-solving info guide instead of another sales pitch. Everyone wins.

The point is that you can and should apply/combine virtually all of my strategies to Google Adwords & Facebook advertising. You'll hit the jackpot. Good luck!

Lesson #31 - Get On TV

Getting free PR on TV is considered a highly difficult feat to achieve. And sure it's challenging, but it's not as hard as you might think.

And TV exposure is incredibly powerful. Getting on any major TV station causes your credibility to skyrocket. Don't get me wrong, putting yourself in front of millions of viewers is tougher than it was 10 or 20 years ago because we now have so many TV channels from which to choose (when I was growing up, we only had three), but people who make it to TV are still perceived as successful experts.

This is due in a large part to the celebrity culture in which we live. We all secretly desire to be associated with celebrities and successful people.

To be clear, it will take much, much more than a simple press release and a phone call to get you on television. Producers and staff alike are bombarded with piles of crap every single day. Your task is to get on the top of pile A. And to do that, you need to be thinking in terms of "What would benefit the viewers of this channel most?" rather than "How can I make a name for myself in the media?"

In a minute, I'll let you in on a secret that can GUARANTEE you TV exposure. But first, you need to have something valuable about which to talk. As I've mentioned in this book more than once, you MUST establish yourself as an expert in your field.

Set yourself apart as the #1 business in your area or market. Become a marketer of valuable problem-solving information. Write a book. Create a free report called "10 Things They Don't Tell You About...," and fill in the blanks. If your writing is crap, get someone to write it for you, but make sure your ideas and thoughts are the ones that go into the report.

Provide valuable advice and information to educate your prospects. You could talk about the cowboys in your industry, and how customers can get a raw deal if they aren't careful. Tell people how to solve problems. Perfect and polish your message, and then get it proofread and printed.

Now you have something to take to the media.

Are you ready for the secret to guaranteeing TV exposure now? Well, take the BBC, for example. The BBC is one of the world's largest and most respected stations (unless you're a Catholic living in Northern Ireland, that is, but I digress).

My point is that if you land any exposure at all on the BBC, you've cracked it. And while you can't buy a slot on the conventional BBC stations, you CAN buy a slot on BBC World. It's not cheap, but consider how much this exposure would boost your credibility and your business.

Then, armed with your 30-second BBC video, you would be well-poised to approach the conventional BBC, ITV, CNN, or any other TV channels and say, "LOOK – here's me on the BBC. Now I'd like to come on your show and give some valuable advice to your viewers."

What do you think your chances of getting on TV for free would be then? Virtually guaranteed if you were persistent and played your cards right. You'd then put your BBC video on your website, of course, and in a DVD to send to ALL your prospects and customers.

Look, 2,000 years or so ago, no one wanted to hear from the wise man standing at the bottom of the hill. They went to hear the wise man standing on the top of the hill. And when you've been on the BBC, that wise man at the top of the hill is YOU!

The question is do you have the balls (or the vagina) to do it? Or are you just too scared? How much money do you REALLY want to make?

When you challenge yourself to go to the very top, you start to discover a lot of things about yourself, and it may not be a very pleasant experience. But, at least you gain an accurate representation of your strengths and weaknesses so you can start improving.

So, go for it. Get yourself on TV. And don't overlook radio either.

Lesson #32 - Add Video to Your Website

Few modern websites have the ability to convert visitors into customers without having a video on the homepage. Think about this for a moment. We've all been conditioned since we were kids to pay attention to the TV... Especially when ads were showing. We've been training our entire lives to get mesmerised by what's on the screen.

And guess what? We act the same when we see a video on a website. As long as the headline of your landing page is relevant to whatever a visitor is seeking, MOST people will click and watch the video.

The downside, of course, is that they can very easily leave your site in just one click, too, so your video has to be engaging, snappy, and interesting. And never, EVER boring. Make your video as professional as possible, with a clear picture and quality audio. Just make sure it doesn't look like a cheap homemade job ... even if it is!

There are a number of ways to pull off this strategy.

Create a TV-type video, where you talk about your products and services. This is usually a bad idea.

Here's a better strategy. Create a video of you, the business owner, telling your story, taking about your staff, and explaining why you're different. This works much better because it lets your prospects and customers see that you're a real, sincere human being with a personality – not a faceless, boring stripy-suited show-off from some big corporation!

Or how about a FANTASTIC way to do this? Use your video to educate your market on how to solve problems, offering free advice with a strong Call-to-Action at the end of the video.

This could also incorporate strategy number two for full effect. The Call-to-Action offers a FREE email course and a FREE DVD/Info Pack via the post, covering both educational material and information about your company. This way, you educate your customers and all the things they need to know before they make a buying decision. And it positions you as the expert in your industry.

By the way, this is a solid launch-point for building your prospect list so you can develop and maintain a relationship with them forever. Later on, you can offer new products and services you haven't even created yet, just like I do with my list. Most businesses don't have any video on their website at all.

Lesson #33 - Understand What Business You're Really In

Are the basic foundations of your business in place? You'd be surprised how many business owners don't actually know what business they're in! I'm not joking. Shouldn't this be the first thing you establish before investing time, effort, and money setting up a business?

It's actually not as easy as you may think to understand what business you're in, even if you've been operating your company for years.

Let me explain.

Most accountants, for example, think they're in the accountancy business, and most plumbers think are in the plumbing business. Actually, they're not!

If you ask these professionals what "THEY DO," they will reply, "Accountant," "Plumber," and so on. Sorry, wrong again.

What if instead they replied with something like, *"I help small businesses save money, avoid unnecessary tax bills, and manage their finances to help increase their profits."* Your response would probably be, *"Bugger me! How do you do that?"* Right?

That's a great deal more impressive than saying, *"Erm, I'm an accountant."* And it gets a conversation going!

A plumber could say, *"I prevent serious water damage in homes by inspecting the plumbing and fixing problems BEFORE they happen, which stops you from having to EVER deal with expensive and damaging water leaks."* (I just made that up on the spot, but you get the picture.)

"Really! How do you do that?"

There isn't a business school or MBA course in the world that teaches this stuff. I learned the hard way. And now I'm telling you, don't bore people to death by telling them your job title. They didn't ask what your title was; they asked, "WHAT DO YOU DO," which really means, *"What can you do for me?"* Or, *"What problems can you solve for me?"*. So, what do you do?

Lesson #34 - The Incredible Power of Customer Testimonials

Testimonials are an extremely powerful force when it comes driving more sales. Your prospects and customers believe what others have to say about you much more than what you have to say about yourself.

We live in a skeptical world... much, much more than it was even five or ten years ago. You can thank the bankers, corporations, politicians, and Catholic priests for destroying any trust we ever had in authority and big businesses.

Hey, I don't normally spend my time blaming others; I just want to identify the problem so I can work on the solution. And the solution is GENUINE testimonials from existing customers. Video testimonials work far better than written ones, but why not use both?

One of my old training websites had over 75 video testimonials and over 50 written ones. All 100% genuine. Our competitors, in contrast, had two or three on their site, all of which were questionable.

You need to inspire your customers and blow your competitors out of the water with a preponderance of proof. And to get that done, nothing beats plastering your site with dozens of genuine testimonials from satisfied customers. On the other hand, nothing will ruin your business faster than **faked** versions.

Spot the dodgy testimonial below:

Testimonial #1: *"[Acme company] are fantastic, The customer service and staff are a credit to the company. I will be contacting all my friends today to strongly recommend [Acme company]." - P. Smith, UK*

Testimonial #2: *"I thoroughly enjoyed my time earning my certificate with [Acme Company] and have met some fantastic people who I hope to keep in touch with for the rest of my life. The staff in Jane, Damian, Michaella and the others were fantastic people who deserve all the credit for being so patient, helpful and fun to be around. I can honestly say, hand on heart, the only thing that could have been improved is that it could have lasted longer so I could have savoured and enjoyed the experience for just one more week...Thank you all so, so much!" - Phil Smith, London, England.*

Which one is more believable? Which one was likely written by the company owner, writing the words they WISHED people would write about them?

This example is pretty obvious, but not all dodgy testimonials are not so easy to spot. One dead give-away can be found in the numbers. No one in the world can be bothered to write 20 to 50 dodgy testimonials that have any chance of fooling anyone. They can easily write two or three though.

Probably the most ridiculous dodgy testimonial ever written!

I saw this a while back on a website called efax® that allows you to send faxes from an email account. I have no idea why anyone would use this service in the first place. I mean, I CAN certainly understand sending a fax to a fax machine, which beeps and demands attention so it gets read right away. I wish everyone still had fax machines. But sending a "fax" by email to another email inbox, as an attachment, is bloody pointless!

Anyhow, their homepage testimonial, which has since been removed, went something like this (I'm paraphrasing here, but I assure you it was this bad):

"Efax is amazing. I use efax to fax all my receipts to myself so I have an online digital archive." -Claire McDontexist, USA

By the way, every fax you send via eFax costs around $0.30 or more.

I sent an email to efax. *"Dear Efax. Why the fuck would anyone want to spend a fortune faxing their receipts to themselves when they can easily scan them in for free?"*

They didn't respond – imagine that. But the testimonial was replaced a few weeks later with another less iffy one.

Contact all your best customers and ask them to write you a testimonial, and make it a policy regularly to request them from here on out. Plaster them all over your website, along with a photo for further social proof.

Lesson#35 - Make the Most of Skype Video Calls

Time is the most valuable commodity you have. When I discovered I could interview potential staff and customers with a Skype video call, I realised this was going to be the BEST EVER time-saving system invented.

Nothing is more time-consuming, frustrating, and a right pain in the arse than having to sit through endless hours interviewing people face to face. Now that the internet is up to speed in most countries, and Skype finally seems to be getting its act together, too, there's no need to endure this torture any longer.

Using tools like scheduleonce.com (I recommend this one, but there are plenty others available), I can easily create a shortlist of candidates and send them a booking link to reserve a 30-minute time slot with me.

I then interview five or six candidates via Skype video and arrange for one or two to come and meet the old-fashioned way. Not only do I save my time, but I save them from spending time and money traveling for the interview – it's a win/win for everyone. And at least those who get rejected find out within five minutes of the video call!

You can also use this to streamline communications with your prospects and customers. If you can, get them on a video call as soon as possible. A genuine connection will happen must faster, and it becomes much more difficult for them to say no.

Lesson #36 - Conferences & Trade Shows

Apart from attending my mastermind groups, this isn't something I like to do much. There are, however, many industries where attending conferences and trade shows can make or break your business.

If that applies to your industry, use the follow-up systems detailed in this book to stay in touch with new contacts, clients, or prospects. Plug them into an automated email sequence and get in touch with them on a daily basis (or at least three times per week) to give them useful, interesting information and tell them your story. Few people ever take the time.

Lesson #37 - Send Bulky Mail

We talked a lot earlier about the power of direct mail. Bulky mail is even better! There's a great story about a brilliant direct marketer who FedExed a sales letter to 50 of the top CEOs in New York. He was selling a high-end investment service, and he wasn't playing around. So, he sent his FedEx letter, and then he followed it with another letter ten days later. Then, he sent a FINAL NOTICE letter ten days after that.

That's three FedEx letters in 30 days!

What happened? He booked five appointments to go and meet with CEOs of these business giants. That's a very good conversion rate, by the way, of 10%. I believe he closed two of the five as well, so a 40% conversion to sale rate.

Brilliant!

But he was unsatisfied with his results from the other 45 CEOs, so he decided to do something different. What'd he do? He sent each of them a wastepaper basket with a letter inside.

That's right...a bloody WASTEPAPER BASKET!

The letter said something like, *"As you're obviously not reading my letters, I thought I would send you a bin to discard them in. My offer closes in three days. Call me now..."*

With that letter, he got another fifteen appointments and closed twelve more sales!!! That's a 28% sales conversion rate from a direct mail campaign – insane!

A lot of people people call this type of thing unprofessional, crazy, or stupid. They say things like, *"This would never work in my business."*

Bullshit! It works. And no one else has the balls to do it, so go ahead and dare to be different.

Lesson #38 - Add Bonuses to Drive the Sale

The amazing secret about bonuses that no one will tell you about, and to which customers will never admit, is that a lot of folks will actually buy your product or service just to get the bloody bonus! It's crazy but absolutely true.

A few years ago, I sold a high-end coaching package for $19,950 (£12,995) per year. The bonus was a brand new MacBook Air computer. After my clients sent over their payment, guess what the first question was?

"When will my website be ready?" Nope.
"What are the arrangements for the training seminar?"

Nope. You guessed it – it was, "When am I getting my free MacBook Air?"

A MacBook Air costs around $1,000 (£600), and the coaching program was selling for $19,950 (£12,995). Do you think it was worth it? Add bonuses to your product or services. Not cheap and nasty stuff like free maps, pens, or coffee mugs but valuable and desirable items people will look forward to. If you're stuck for ideas, throw in a two-bottle gift box of French wine with a quality bottle opener. You can't go wrong there.

Lesson #39 - Write a Book

"My mother once suggested that I write a story to relieve the boredom when I was sick and I told her I didn't know how. 'How do you know if you've never tried?" she asked." - Agatha Christie

I mentioned before that you need to position yourself as an expert in your field, and writing a book is one of the best ways of doing this. Which do you think would impress a prospect or customer more – you handing over your business card or a copy of your book?

You're probably thinking, "I can't write a book. I'm not a good writer." Or, "I don't have the time." And various other excuses. Well, believe that if it makes you feel better, but consider this.

A 200-page book, with roughly 200 words per page comes to 40,000 words. That's 1,000 words per day for 40 days. In other words, if you just sat down and wrote for one to two hours per day for five weeks, you'd have your book!

If you think your writing is crap, well, how do you know? Have you really put out the effort? Okay, then hire someone on elance.com to ghostwrite it for you if it's really that bad – again, just be sure your thoughts and ideas are the ones that go into it.

Personally, I don't recommend this method because I believe that everyone has what it takes to write a book – YOU should write it and THEN get it proofread and edited. But ghostwriting is definitely better than not producing one at all.

Your competitors are probably never going to write a book, which means you should.

Lesson #40 - Call Your Unconverted Leads

I'll make this a quick one. Go back and call all your unconverted leads and ask them what problems they need solving right now. Then give them a solution. Just ask; you'll be amazed what this can dredge up! Show an interest in helping them rather than trying to sell them something. Again, hardly anyone does this. Be different.

Lesson #41 - Go Niche

People prefer to buy from companies that focus on their needs. They respond more, pay more, and stick around longer if your company is niche. It's much better, for example, to be a tyre/exhaust garage than a general, "we fix everything," garage.

Don't just sell shoes. Sell shoes for tall or short men or women. A clothes shop for fat people would go down well in the USA, though you'd probably want to call it something else!

Don't open an Italian restaurant; open a vegan Italian restaurant. Or, how about a vegetarian-only pizza joint? I bet if you opened one in the most affluent or funky suburb in the UK, you'd be swamped.

Selling life insurance? Aye, so is everyone else. How about selling life insurance to 40-year-old divorced women living in Edinburgh? Or, suppose you were a soap maker who invented a product to gently remove chlorine from swimmers' hair? There's a guy in the USA who sells marketing coaching programs to carpet cleaners and to no one else!

Ditch your least profitable products and services, and then focus on the 20% that bring in the cash. Then, craft your USP and make it your laser-targeted message to the niche market.

Lesson #42 - Re-Marketing

Re-marketing means you keep marketing again and again to people who have visited your website. And it works miracles.

Here's how it's done. Set up highly-targeted banner ad campaigns online with a company like outbrain.com or advertise.com. When someone visits your website, you MUST get their name and email address. You might even want to ask for the postal address and phone number, preferably in exchange for a small free gift.

Then, send useful, interesting information by email and post, like a problem-solving guide or interesting news about the latest rip-off in your industry. DO NOT send crap like *"20% off if you buy now,"* because people HATE this kind of stuff.

Your re-marketing ads will follow your visitors and hot leads around the internet for months, making it seem like you are everywhere! This is good for your credibility and your bottom line.

As the Wolf of Wall Street famously said, *"Don't stop selling until they either buy or die,"*

Lesson #43 - Combine Online & Offline Marketing Strategies

Look for ways to combine your online marketing strategies with your offline marketing.

For example, when you send a direct mail shot by post, ask your prospects to visit your website and take some form of action. Then deliver your product by post. When someone signs up on your website, send them a free report in the mail.

An ad in the local newspaper, or trade-mag, should run alongside a re-marketing banner-ad campaign online. Thus, when people see your offline ad, they then visit your website and a banner ad follows them around the internet for weeks. A few days later, they receive a postcard in the mail, followed by a phone call from one of your advisors.

Your company now appears to be everywhere, and they can't help but consider you the authority in the marketplace. They may not be ready to buy just yet, but when they are ready to buy, you can bet you'll be the first name about which they think.

Your combined marketing campaigns compound on each other, and each marketing funnel supports and feeds all the others. Are you starting to get the picture?

Lesson #44 - Shock & Awe

"Marketing is a contest for people's attention."
- Seth Godin

I told you a story earlier about the guy who sent a wastepaper BIN in the post to a highly targeted list of CEOs. It's a brilliant shock-and-awe tactic few business owners have the guts to pull off. Shock-and-awe marketing separates you from your competitors.

Another famous marketing story is about the accountant in the United States. When someone called his office or visited his website, he sent a shock-and-awe package in the post that consisted of a free info guide on how he could legally save their business a fortune in unnecessary taxes and show them how to slash costs.

The shock-and-awe part was that the info guide arrived in one of those big A4 continuous paper boxes. At the top was the info guide and a sales letter. The other 250 sheets of paper were testimonials from satisfied customers!

Nothing else!

Of course, few people would ever bother to read so many testimonials, if anyone, but it doesn't matter. Job done!

Shock and awe simply means you send something that was totally unexpected and leaves them feeling pleasantly surprised and extremely interested. How many accountants do you know that practice such brilliant marketing?

Don't fall into the "my business is different" trap. If an accountant can get away with this outrageous shit, and become very rich in the process, so can you!

Lesson #45 - Create a Powerful USP

What is your USP (Unique Selling Proposition)?

Most business owners can't answer this, and it's one of the most fundamental questions in business.

Your USP needs to clarify why you are different from everyone else in the market place in just a few seconds. It should be unique, desirable, short, and specific. And there are certain questions a USP must answer within a few seconds.

"Why should I do business with you over every other business in the marketplace? What problems can you solve for me? What guarantees do you offer?"

The most common, and stupid, responses to the USP question are:

1. **"We offer great service."** This one is totally crap. Offering great service is what customers expect as bog standard. Why are you *different* than everyone else? Why should I do business with YOU?

2. **"We care about our customers."** No, you don't – piss off. Everyone says that, and we don't believe you! What can you offer to PROVE TO US THAT YOU CARE?

3. **"Find our product cheaper anywhere else and we'll match the price."** So, you're the cheapest then? Does that also mean you're the crappiest? Competing on price is okay if you want quick sales from bad customers, but it's horrible positioning. 85% of people don't want cheap; they want good value!

Remember the story about Domino's Pizza? It created one of the best USPs ever, and it launched a multi-million dollar business in a crowded marketplace. It identified a BIG problem in the pizza delivery business, and its USP answer to that problem was: **"Fresh, hot pizza delivered to your door in 30 minutes or less, guaranteed or it's free."**

The USP doesn't mention how good the pizza is, just that it will arrive on time, fresh and hot. No mention of Mama's traditional recipe or how long the company has been in business. A specific time promise and a strong guarantee – and that's it.

Wake up! Nobody gives a toss about you, your company, your qualifications, or how long you've been in business. What Domino's understood is that people only care about themselves and what you can do for them TODAY. Figure that out, and profit!

Lesson #46 - Ask For the Order

Some business owners and salespeople are actually scared to ask for the order because they fear rejection. They can chat all day long and do a pretty good job presenting their products and services, but they fail miserably when it comes to closing the deal. Are you one of those?

Or, sometimes they do ask, but their body language betrays them. Their tone of voice exposes lack of confidence in the product and the price. A good salesperson pounces. Even a customer saying "I'll think about it" becomes a golden opportunity – offer to throw in a free "something" if they order NOW!

Listen in on your salespeople to discover how many times they ask for the order. Even the most experienced often still fall into this trap of "not asking."

What to do about it? Ask three times and get three NOs before giving up. Then call back the next day and ask another three times. I guarantee this will boost your sales!

Lesson #47 - Develop a Millionaire Mindset

"By unlinking your money motivation from anger, fear, and the need to prove yourself, you can install new connections for earning your money, such as contribution, purpose, and joy." - T Harv Ecker

If you're struggling financially or always appear to have cash flow problems, it's because you've developed a set of limiting beliefs over the years about money and wealth, most of which are simply not true.

These false beliefs are holding you back.

When someone claims they doesn't agree with my philosophy on money and/or wealth, or that "money is not important," I immediately know two important things about that person.

They're broke. They will always be broke, unless he/she changes beliefs about money and wealth.

It's very likely that your upbringing has ingrained negative beliefs about money into your subconscious mind. This applies to most of us. I'd guess that around 80% of the population of any western country has a negative set of beliefs about money, and around 20% has a moderately or exceptionally-positive set of beliefs.

Do those figures ring a bell? Remember the 80/20 rule? How many times did you hear the expressions below in your childhood? *"Money doesn't grow on trees, you know."* *"What do you think I am, made of money?"*

How many times did you hear your parents argue over money? One of the most common excuses people have is,

"My health is much more important than my money." There is certainly a lot of truth to this. After all, what's the point of having money if you're in such poor health that you can't enjoy it?

But most people are in good health and they're still broke.! Ask yourself this: how healthy would you be if you had absolutely no money?... If you didn't have cash for food, medication, or a roof over your head? But, *"I just want enough to get by."* Really? So, why are you still buying lottery tickets then?

Here's another one you've probably heard. *"Money is the root of all evil."* Ouch – stings a little, doesn't it? But this is actually a misquote. It was originally, *"The love of money is the root of all evil."* Similar statements but two completely different meanings! The correct one certainly has some truth in it.

It's no wonder that deep, deep down in your psyche there are a number of negative beliefs that say, "Having lots of money is not good."

When was the last time you heard someone say something positive about money like this?

"Money buys hospitals, schools, food, and shelter. Money buys medicine, research, and technology to improve the health and well-being of millions of people around the world. Money is hope, joy, and fulfilment. Money rescues people from poverty, and the lack of money keeps them in it.

"Money alone may not buy happiness, but money can buy something FAR more valuable than money, or even your health. Money buys TIME. Time is the MOST valuable commodity we have on this planet, and it's in very limited supply for every one of us. Money buys you the TIME to spend with your family and loved ones.

"Money buys you the freedom from the job you hate. Money lets you spend your time on the things you love doing. Traveling, reading, singing, dancing, scuba diving, driving, playing music, relaxing, playing, thinking, sleeping, having sex, sharing, giving, and more."

"Money lets you help those people who don't have any!"

Money doesn't make you happy. It just makes MORE of who you already are.

Let me say that again! Money doesn't make you happy. It just makes MORE of who you already are. I mentioned this earlier in this book, but it's really important to go over it again. If you're greedy, you become greedier. If you're selfish, then you'll be more selfish. If you're generous, then you become even MORE generous. If you're happy, then you'll be MUCH happier.

If you're fat, you'll become OBESE. And if you drink too much or take too many drugs, then having more money will probably kill you.

You need to change your habits and your beliefs before you can start to makes lots of money in your business. After all, how can you possibly get rich if you believe money isn't important? Or that it's bad?

By the way, perhaps you subconsciously think that you'd feel guilty about becoming rich when those around you are not.

Because the truth is when you become really wealthy, it actually says a lot more about your peers than it does about you. Discovering those who resent you for it reveals who your true friends are. And that's great information to have.

For now, don't worry about it. You need to figure out who YOU are first and determine which limiting beliefs are holding you back. I could dedicate a whole book to this subject on money and the mindset. For now, I strongly recommend you read *"Secrets of the Millionaire Mind," by T. Harv Ekker.*

If you're really committed to improving your financial status, this book is an absolute must.

Lesson #48 - Create a Smartphone App

Smartphone apps are fantastic media tools for every business, small or large. It's just brilliant to be able to find whatever you need with a few quick swipes instead of searching on Google or poring through a badly-organised website. That kind of cumbersome searching used to piss me off no end when searching for football scores and news updates.

Another big peeve of mine is how email is still so unreliable. I mean, why on earth is it that you can't send a simple email to someone with 100% certainty it will arrive there safely? And why do we still have to deal with spam? It's very simple; I only want to receive messages from the addresses that I approve, and everyone else's goes into a quarantine folder.

And there's nothing I hate worse than people not receiving my important emails or asking me to resend it because they can't find it. AAARRGGH!!!

I was so pissed off about email problems that I created my own app, called eTelex, which allows users to send important files and documents with 100% guaranteed delivery and security. Zero spam and zero phishing. eTelex also allows people electronically to sign a document and notify the sender with a click, an action that makes the document legally binding.

As far as I'm concerned, important files, documents, and certain messages should NEVER be lumped in with all the other email, spam, and annoying chats your receive around the clock. When someone sends you an eTelex, you better read it now because it's bloody important!

I'll let you know when beta testing is finished and it goes live.

When you create a good app for your business, you can solve your most frustrating problems. You can communicate and deliver information directly to your prospects and customers the way YOU want to. And if it works well, you can always take it to the market!

Get an app built for your business today. Search Google for App Builder or App Maker to get started.

Lesson #49 - Get Good at Public Speaking

Speaking at local and international events can position you as an expert in your field. Unfortunately, speaking in front of a group is just about everyone's biggest fear. Or more precisely, making an arse of one's self in front of a group of people is everyone's worst nightmare. Most people would rather have their nipples melted with a blow torch!

But you know what else that means? A lower barrier to entry. Make the effort to learn and practice the art of public speaking and you'll get better at it as you grow more confidence. You become the expert, and your competitors start to seem like the amateurs in comparison. You become the wise man at the top of the mound. Up for the challenge? It's your choice.

Lesson #50 - Exercise Every Day

Right now you're probably starting to wonder if I'm cutting corners on the 52 marketing strategies because I'm running out of ideas... right?

I was going to dedicate this chapter to online banner ads. But you know what? None of the banner ads we tested brought in any customers. Same goes for my clients. So, it may be worth a blast in your sector. But in our experience, they simply do NOT work.

SO lets talk about something much more productive. I'm not joking when I say that incorporating the daily habit of exercise does wonders for both your health AND your wealth.

You sleep better, eat better, work better, and think better. You make better decisions, and you have the zest and energy to face the day's challenges. Exercise also improves your sex life and releases stress. And let's face it, if you're not having sex at least three times per week, then there's definitely room for improvement!

I train in Muay Thai kickboxing about two to three times in a good week ... and man, is it tough! I also go to the gym once or twice a week and do a little swimming on the weekends. I feel great! And it shows in my work.

Try it for a month, and watch how everything in your life magically starts to change for the better.

Lesson #51 - Travel Abroad and Discover New Ideas

"The world is a book and those who do not travel read only one page." - Augustine of Hippo

I still find it hard to believe that I live in an amazing, vibrant Asian city and spend half the year on a beautiful tropical Island in the Gulf of Thailand. How the hell did I end up here?

Sometimes I miss certain things from back home in Scotland. Hilarious family and friends. The big Scottish breakfast with haggis, real sausages, and a lovely cup of tea (it just doesn't taste the same anywhere else). The fresh air, the music, Irn Bru, and weekend drives up to Loch Lomond. Being able to speak at the right speed!

One thing I definitely do NOT miss though, is the bloody WEATHER! Especially over the past few years, with all those severe winter storms battering the country into the ground. I've become spoiled by the tropics, and I just can't stand the cold wind and rain anymore.

You only get a real perspective on your home country once you've been away from it for a while! That's when you start to realise where you truly want to be and who you really are. In my case, I left Scotland in 1999, and I never went back home to settle. Sure, I travel there a few times a year on business, but that's about it.

I now happily spend my time in either Singapore, Hong Kong, Koh Samui, or Bangkok with my beautiful Thai wife and our two amazing young daughters. If you asked me where my home is now, I'd say it's right here in Asia.

Listen, if you had told me all those years ago I'd end up living in Asia with a Thai wife and kids, I would have said you were barking mad! But when you take a year, or even a few months, to live overseas, it changes you profoundly. In fact, wouldn't have become the successful business man I am had I stayed at home.

After spending a few months abroad, you eventually make one of two choices:

1. You go back home with a whole new outlook on your life and your business after an amazing period of self-discovery.

2. You decide to start a whole new life and a new business abroad, and you stay there for good (with regular visits back home, of course).

Either way, it changes you forever. Whatever you decide to do in your life, spend some time traveling abroad, and by traveling, I don't mean lying on a beach or getting pissed in Spain for two weeks. I promise you it will be THE best decision you EVER make in your entire life. For me, the idea of never leaving Scotland just doesn't bear thinking about! If you can't take a year off at this stage in your life, then fine. But that's still no excuse for not travelling and trying new things as much as possible. Go spend a week in the slums of Calcutta. Visit Machu Pichu. Sail around Sydney Harbour.

Go skydiving or bungy-jumping in New Zealand. Get a soapy massage in Bangkok. Get your arse out of that dreary shithole of a place you live in for a while and start living. This could very well be the best 'idea & money' generator in this whole book!

Lesson #52 - Implement

"It doesn't matter if you've failed or if you've been beaten. All that matters is that you learn something, get back up, and try again. Because winning is a good feeling, but winning when nobody else thought you could is an awesome feeling." - Unknown

Congratulations! You are now a sales and marketing expert, and a successful businessperson in the making. You will never be at the mercy of Google, Social Media, or Advertising sales reps ever again. However, all the brilliant marketing strategies and success secrets in the world don't mean a thing if you don't implement them.

There's no point in buying a nice expensive car if you're not going to drive the thing. It won't run itself, and you'll get zero benefit or joy out of staring at it. If there's ONE secret of success then it's simply this. Implementation!

All you have to do is what 95% of people reading this book will NOT do. Implement what you've learnt. Of course, you don't need to implement all 52 steps, but aim to add twelve new marketing strategies or funnels and watch how your business improves drastically.

Stop pissing around on Facebook, YouTube, and all those free porn websites and start implementing right NOW.

I wish you all the very best of joy and success.

Last Word:

Every time New Year's comes around, people make resolutions about the things they're going to change. Lose weight, start a new hobby, stop smoking, get laid more, and the list goes on. Little do they know, they have ZERO chance of achieving these goals. Why?

Because they're focusing on the wrong things.

Trying to change habits built over a lifetime by willpower alone is crazy. It rarely works. Listen carefully to what those around you (and probably you too) actually say when talking about new resolutions.

It goes something like this:

- "I'm really going to try to lose weight this year."
- "I'm really going to try to make more money this year."
- "I'm really going to try to…"

See a pattern? The key word here is "TRY."

When you TRY something, it's usually bound to fail. Even if you start with total commitment and discipline (which 99% of people do not have), it still doesn't work. And when you inevitably fail, then you feel GUILTY about making future attempts, which are now even more likely to fail.

Tony Robbins explains that any success or failure is a self-perpetuating circle of four main elements.

Thoughts lead to Feelings lead to Actions lead to Results lead to Thoughts ...And around and around you go. So, when you stick a "positive" or "negative" in front of any one of these words, it affects the whole cycle.

Negative thoughts create negative feelings, which create negative actions, which ultimately produce shit results. Those results then create more negative thoughts, and so on...

When you have positive thoughts, on the other hand, you create positive feelings, which create positive actions, and ultimately positive results. Then you have more positive thoughts based on the positive results, and so on...

So, don't TRY to do anything this year or you will set yourself up for more failure. Instead, rearrange things and put systems in place.

For example:

If you really want to lose weight, give your car to someone for a month and walk to work. Or, use the stairs everyday instead of the lift. Don't keep carbs or sweets in your fridge, so you won't be tempted to eat them.

If you want to read more, wrap your TV in some bubble wrap and stick it in the garage. If you want to drink less, or stop altogether then stop hanging out with people who like to drink. If you want to stop smoking, don't buy the bloody things in the first place. Ban smoking in your house and office.

If you want more time to work ON your business, or more time to spend with your kids, hire a PA to handle 80% of your daily tasks.

If you want to make more money, implement at least some of the steps I am sharing with you in this course.

Start with these 5 steps right NOW

1. Hire a PA to handle your emails, Facebook management, general admin tasks, and just about everything else other than marketing and the bank account. Conduct Skype interviews first before arranging face-to-face interviews, so you can weed out the obvious deadbeats.

2. Turn your website into a lead-generating magnet, and then implement multiple follow-ups via email, direct mail, phone call, or whatever works for you.

3. Raise your prices by 50% and/or create a premium product or service.

4. Offer an outrageous, unconditional money-back guarantee, and honour it.

5. Send a nice gift-wrapped bottle of wine to all your customers after each sale, or at least every month if your order value doesn't warrant the expense. If you're on the fence about this, imagine how they'll feel about you. Envision how much they will talk about you, buy more from you, and refer you to friends just based on that monthly bottle of wine!

Getting the 80/20 DONE is one of the most productive ways to add more to your bottom line. So, instead of sitting around all day talking about all the things you want to do.

I am keen to hear about your successes and challenges after implementing some of these new strategies & systems so send me some feedback at jimmycrangle@me.com. Don't write to say to disagree with me, or that you tried some of my suggestions and it didn't work. I'm not interested in hearing from whiners, moaners and those who give up so easily.

Thank you very much for your time and I wish you every success in your business and in your life.

About Jimmy Crangle

Jimmy Crangle grew up in Coatbridge, just outside of Glasgow, Scotland. An independent marketing consultant, author, and coach, Jimmy is becoming quite a buzz in the marketing world. He specialises in teaching entrepreneurs, business owners, and CEOs highly-effective marketing strategies. He personally coaches them and shows them the fastest, easiest path to success. His business is now growing at such a rate that he is very selective in choosing his customers.

Jimmy now spends most of his time in South East Asia and the UK. He is happily married to a beautiful Thai woman with two young daughters.

As a premium member of Perry Marshall's roundtable, Dan Kennedy's Inner Circle and Chris Cardell's mastermind club, Jimmy is well connected to the world's leading marketing brains.

About Me by Me

Let me give you an honest bio about myself and how I got where I am today. I was born in a working class area of Coatbridge, Scotland. I spent most of my childhood really confused about things. I had a few troubled adolescent years from 15 to 17, despite having well-meaning parents. For the most part, our family – which also consisted of my older sister, older brother, and younger sister – was fairly stable as far as families go, and there weren't too many family dramas to contend with.

16 Years Old - I Started Playing the Bass Guitar

I got kicked out of school at 16 for being absent too often. That's when I started playing bass guitar and joined a local band. The singer's (Tony) dad was a millionaire, and all the other band members – Martin, Mark, and Gerry – were attending university or holding down good jobs.

This was a big eye opener for me. I realised these intelligent guys and their rich families were not really much different from the people with whom I was used to hanging out. But there were some key differences. Clearly, they had better money-management skills, for one, and it soon became obvious they had a far more positive outlook and didn't see any need to get drunk at every opportunity.

In the housing scheme where I was brought up, most people were pretty negative about the idea of education or "doing well." My new friends had real ambitions in life, and I felt it starting to rub off on me.

My photo ended up in the local paper for playing bass at a charity gig. I loved the feeling of being recognised locally and feeling important for actually doing something good. The moment of fame also led to my first proper sexual encounter with my then girl friend, arguably the best-looking girl in the school.

It's amazing how quickly a piece of local fame can remove a girl's underwear. I'd been trying for ages before that.

18 Years Old - Selling Clothes Pegs and Ironing Board Covers Door-to-Door

I don't remember why the band broke up, but I was gutted. I honestly thought we were going to be rich and famous. In fact, I still pull out the demos from time to time for a listen, and we were pretty good for a bunch of 16-year-old kids. In any case, I continued to play bass as a hobby while I went from one crap job to another, but my dream of the spotlight was over.

An old friend, Brian Docherty, introduced me to the world of direct selling and asked me to join the sales team. That following week I was out knocking on doors, selling dishcloths, clothes pegs, ironing board covers, and general household crap. We actually did pretty well, pulling in around £200 quid a week, which was a small fortune at the time. Brian was always the top salesperson on the bus, and I was always a close second. I could never beat the bastard!

But actually, I soon became quite happy with my performance and being number two. At least I knew where the benchmark was. I learnt a lot about selling, about myself, and about other people going door to door. Many of the principles I learnt back then, in fact, still apply today in online and offline marketing.

One thing I noticed was that the worst salespeople on the bus were generally negative and liked to blame everything else they could think up for their poor results. I quickly saw it was all about attitude and had nothing to do with the quality of the customers or the weather.

I lasted about eight or nine months, and then I decided to pack it in. The important life lessons I picked up doing that work stayed with me to this day.

22 Years Old - I Became One of the World's First Ever Spammers

At 22, I landed a job with a company that sold and maintained Telex machines. Remember those old clunky things? To refresh your memory, telex was the first ever popular electronic mail system used mainly by large corporations and banks. It was secure, reliable, outdated and expensive.

It turned out the telex industry was nearing extinction, but we didn't know it yet; there were still hundreds of large firms relying on them for important communications.

Anyhow, there were only two or three companies still in the market at this point. The one I worked for went bust, and that's when I started my own telex company with one of the other salesmen I worked with.

It was the easiest money we had ever made. Most companies were still using antiquated machines, so we offered upgrades free of charge. Whatever they were paying to British telecom, they could simply pay the same amount to us on a three- to five-year contract.

And how did we target the market? By telex, of course. We had the telex directory, and we spammed everyone in the book. Of course, we didn't call it spam back then because such a thing didn't yet exist. We just considered it a cold call.

See, telex messages are never ignored because the machine starts beeping when a message comes in. So, we advised telex users that most old telex machines weren't year 2000 compliant and we offered a free upgrade. Even if their machines were compliant, the customers usually upgraded anyways. British Telecom pulled out of the market around that time, and we made a bloody fortune.

There never has been, and never will be, a more highly-targeted direct mail system. One that offered 100% delivery to a highly-specific target market. So, there you go – I was one of the world's first ever email spammers, and I didn't even know it.

I could write a whole book about my life, but I think I've said enough for now. I'll leave the rest for book number two.... if it ever gets written.

Thank you for your time!

===============

You can contact me at: jimmycrangle@me.com I won't reply to every email, especially the ones from nutters, whiners, losers and generally negative people. But if you have something positive to say, or you have some feedback on how this book has helped you, then I look forward to hearing from you.

###

www.ingramcontent.com/pod-product-compliance
Lightning Source LLC
Chambersburg PA
CBHW070028210526
45170CB00012B/360